# THE
# GOLFER'S
# BIBLE

Frank Kenyon Allen

# THE
# GOLFER'S
# BIBLE

**Co-authored by Tom Lo Presti,
Dale Mead and Barbara Romack**

DOUBLEDAY & COMPANY, INC., GARDEN CITY, NEW YORK

ISBN: 0-385-01402-3
LIBRARY OF CONGRESS CATALOG CARD NUMBER 68-11788
COPYRIGHT © 1968 BY FRANK KENYON ALLEN, TOM LO PRESTI,
DALE MEAD AND BARBARA ROMACK
ALL RIGHTS RESERVED
PRINTED IN THE UNITED STATES OF AMERICA
20   19   18   17

*The authors fully acknowledge and appreciate the use
of the format and techniques described in the booklet
titled, "Pocket Golf Tips," produced by Golf Digest, Inc.,
and issued with a subscription to their excellent Golf
Digest Magazine.*

# ACKNOWLEDGMENTS

My sincere thanks to Woodrow "Woody" Hutchison, Athletic Director of the American River College, Sacramento, California, for his counsel and excellent advice as to the type of instruction material best suited to golf student training.

AND TO:

Mike Korich and Dick Madsack, PGA teaching professionals, for their additional advice regarding the instruction procedure in this manual which would be most helpful for the professional teacher and his students.

AND TO:

My close personal friend, the late Howard Oakes, formerly a well-known commercial artist, for his excellent advice in the preparation and composition of this book.

AND TO:

Ken Morton, assistant head professional, Haggin Oaks Golf Course, at Sacramento, California, for his wholehearted cooperation in furnishing the equipment and other material, together with price ranges, for the section on golf equipment in this book.

To each of these individuals, I am deeply indebted.

FRANK KENYON ALLEN

# THE AUTHORS

## FRANK KENYON ALLEN

Frank Kenyon Allen is now retired, and even though seventy years old, he still enjoys a handicap of ten, and plays golf practically every day. He has played the game for fifty-four years, and gives credit for his good health to his daily round of golf. Because of his love for the game, and his many years of experience, it is his hope, and the hope of the other authors, that this book will contribute something of real value to help every golfer both young and old who may be needing good basic instruction.

## TOM LO PRESTI

Recognized as one of the finest teachers of the game, "Tommy" Lo Presti has devoted thirty-six years of his life to the task of helping others to learn the fine points of the game of golf. Many of these have gone on to win local championships. He has been head professional at Haggin Oaks Golf Course in Sacramento, California, for thirty-three years. A Class A member of PGA, he was voted National PGA Club Pro in 1962.

## BARBARA ROMACK

In 1953 Barbara Romack won the Canadian Amateur crown, and in 1954 the U. S. Women's Amateur Championship. The following year she was the runner-up for the British Women's Amateur. As a professional, she won the Leesburg Open in 1960, then finished in the runner-up spot in the Women's Western Open, losing a playoff to Joyce Ziske. In 1965, she was elected president of the Ladies Professional Golf Association.

As a consultant and co-author of this series of instruction sections she is eminently qualified to offer her advice to women golfers in particular and to many of the beginners and high handicap players of the male gender. She is largely responsible for the material in the section, "Our Lady Golfer."

## DALE MEAD

Dale Mead started his career at the Peach Tree Country Club in Marysville, California, and is now head professional at Del Rio Country Club in Modesto, California.

The excellence of his golf shot executions should be evident in the illustrating photos of this book.

# CONTENTS

# INTRODUCTION

This series of golf instruction sections has been prepared primarily for the "beginner" although the techniques described are designed to be equally helpful to the player who has never, or very seldom, ever sought the advantages to be obtained through instruction by a good PGA teaching professional.

Most of the nation's fine high schools and colleges have contributed greatly to the learning progress of today's young golf students. It is an established fact, however, that none of these golf instructors, either in the schools, or in the ranks of teaching professionals, has anything to provide their students except the "physical" golf shot execution training.

This training is valuable without any question. It would be more valuable if the golf instructor had something available that the student could use during his private practice sessions, to keep him from forgetting some of the things the instructor has told him—when he is "on his own."

The sections of this book provide the very thing that is needed. They are designed as a "supplement" to the physical teaching by any good golf instructor. The game of golf cannot be learned from books alone. It takes a combination of physical instruction, supplemented by a sensible, concise chronology of the techniques to be employed, which can be studied and *memorized*. Once these techniques are firmly fixed in the student's mind, their ap-

plications become more or less "automatic" when called upon in actual play.

To aid the student in quickly acquiring this automatic knowledge, the following procedure for exact execution is shown in subsequent pages:

*What to do:* The Technique (step-by-step)
*How to do it:* Photo Illustrations
*Why you do it:* List of Explanations

Study and *memorize* the techniques, then see your golf instructor again, to review what you have learned, and to further improve your golf shot executions. It's an even bet that you will surprise him—and *yourself!* However, while you are in the process of learning the techniques to be employed, from this book or any other, remember that in practicing these techniques, *you* cannot see what you are doing as well as your instructor can when he is watching you during a lesson, so don't try to "go it alone." If the game is worth learning properly—and it is—take lessons *regularly* from a good instructor until you have mastered the techniques. Once mastered, it is doubtful that you will ever forget them.

A good many people have been heard to say, "I don't want to take the game so seriously— I don't want to take the time to study and memorize the techniques." Our answer to that is—O.K., then be satisfied to join the ranks of about 90 percent of the ten million people in the country who very seldom, if ever, score in the eighties, and many of whom never break a hundred.

Our bet is that *you* are different; that you are one of those who have enough pride in yourself to do what is necessary to become one of the topflight players of this game of golf. Try it! and find out how easy it is to quickly become one of the top 10 percent—a low handi-cap golfer whose skill matches his enthusiasm.

It is our firm conviction that there is not one boy or girl, or man or woman, of almost any age (unless a complete invalid) who cannot learn to be a good player of this wonderful game of golf in a relatively short time with the proper instruction and practice. So let's get started! But let's remember to master *one step at a time*. Good luck, and best wishes.

THE AUTHORS

# FOREWORD

Much has been written on the proper techniques to be employed in the execution of various golf shots.

To attempt to incorporate all of the instructional advice necessary for proper performance, starting with proper gripping of club, stance and address, basic swing, wood shots, iron play, trouble shots, and the many other phases of this wonderful game of golf, would require a volume too massive to be practical.

The average golfer needing instructions (and who doesn't) cannot logically absorb all of such valuable instruction at one time. To attempt to do this would only result in utter confusion.

*One step at a time,* starting with the "physical" teaching by a specialist—your golf professional—is accepted as the proper beginning. Next, the player should concentrate on this teaching during practice rounds until he feels he has mastered this *one step* to the best of his ability. Then he should return to his professional for a further review of his performance.

What frequently happens, however, is that the pupil (through his intense desire to concentrate on the instructions from his teacher) often forgets, or misconstrues certain parts of the instruction he or she has received, with the result that faulty execution of the past creeps back in, and the real value of the instruction is virtually lost.

This is one of the reasons why most teaching professionals prefer not to cover more than one subject at a lesson period, to prevent as much confusion as possible. The student, therefore, should also concentrate on one subject at a time and not try to master the whole game at once. It just cannot be done.

What this book attempts to do is provide today's pupil with an easy reference guide, step-by-step, in a simple and concise listing, on each phase of the game separately, as a *supplement* to the instruction he receives from his golf professional. Unlike many books on golf, you don't have to read a whole paragraph to pick out the technique you are seeking.

To get the full value from the steps outlined:

1. *Memorize each point.*
   (How else can your mind contain the proper things to do?)

2. *Practice each step separately.*
   (Until your performance becomes automatic.)

3. *See your professional teacher.*
   (For a review of your proficiency.)

If this procedure is followed, it is reasonable to assume that the pupil will have complete confidence in his ability to execute his golf shots well during actual play, because he will automatically know the proper things to do.

With such confidence, relaxation, so essential to proper execution of all golf shots, is assured.

Remember—if you wish to excel at *anything,* you must *work* at it—systematically.

This section is the first of a series of major phases of the game, starting with the first essential—*the basic swing.*

NOTE: The outline of all execution techniques, as well as photo illustrations, are designed for *right-handed* players. Simply reverse positions for left-handers.

# SECTION ONE

SECTION ONE

# THE BASIC SWING

## THE TEE SHOT

Step 1. *Stance and Address*
Step 2. *The Backswing*
Step 3. *The Downswing*
Step 4. *Impact and Follow-through*

For each step above, a simple chronology of the techniques is outlined, then illustrated, and then each point is explained in subsequent pages. The explanations are for your reference.

Study and *memorize* the simple techniques outlined for each step. Then make up your mind that each time you step up to your ball, you will relax and execute your swing the way your study and practice has helped make it possible.

*Don't worry* or get *all tensed up*. Just do it the best way you can. If you have done your work well, you will be surprised how easily things begin to fall into place.

Your golf instructor will probably start you swinging with a ⚜6 or ⚜7 iron instead of a wood club, because the irons are easier to swing. While we have no quarrel with this practice, however, we have started description of the techniques of the basic swing with the ⚜1 wood or driver.

While the swing with the longer wood clubs is a little more difficult, you won't get to use the shorter irons too often unless you learn to drive the ball off the tee.

## THE STANDARD GRIP

### What to Do

1. Take your grip in the *left* hand first, with the left thumb resting firmly on the upper right side of club handle, and the other fingers (particularly the last three) gripping firmly, *but not tensely,* and seeing that only two or three knuckles show when looking down on this hand.
2. Place your right hand against the club shaft with the palm square to the target, and with the thumb on the *upper left* of the shaft. (*Don't place the thumb straight down on top of the club handle.*)
3. Cradle the club handle *across* the forefinger of right hand, and rest the end of the thumb on this finger. Applying pressure of the thumb and forefinger on the club handle contributes greatly to the feel of a good grip. Also, it helps to assure correct alignment of the club head (square to the target) throughout the entire swing. *Under no circumstances* should you allow the right forefinger to extend loosely against the right side of the shaft, as so many people do. (Amateurs, of course.)
4. Now complete the right-hand grip with the two middle fingers, and *overlap* the forefinger

of the *left* hand with the little finger of the *right* hand. After completing the grip, see that the "Vs" formed between thumbs and forefingers of *both* hands are pointing toward the *right* shoulder.

The above grip must be adjusted for intentional *hook* or *fade* shots, but see your professional teacher first for proper instructions.

Because some golfers' hands are too small or not adapted to the overlapping (Vardon) grip outlined above, see your professional for instructions on the interlocking or the baseball grip.

### How to Do It

LEFT-HAND POSITION

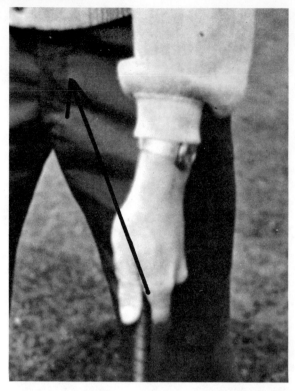

Left-hand position showing "V" pointing to right shoulder.

Grip firmly with last three fingers.

Overlapping grip shown.

## RIGHT-HAND POSITION

Right hand against shaft, palm square to target.

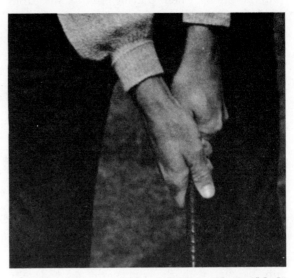

Final position at address, with hands "welded" together. End of right thumb, and tip of right forefinger should touch, with slight pressure of both on club grip.

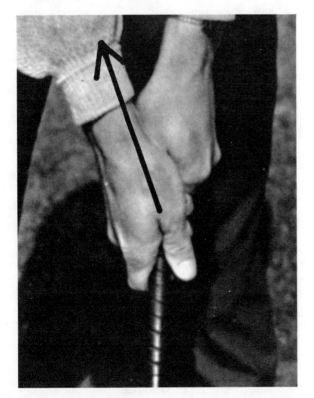

Right-hand position on club grip. Note position of right thumb (to left upper part of grip), *not on top.* Also "V" pointing to right shoulder.

### Why You Do It

ITEM 1. Unless a golfer learns to properly grip his clubs, there is little or no assurance that he will be able to execute good golf shots consistently. Developing a proper grip is the first step in setting up a correct swing pattern.

When the left-hand grip on the club handle allows two or three finger knuckles to be seen by the player, a *strong* grip is created, providing good left-hand control of the club. The "V" formed between the left thumb and forefinger should point toward the *right* shoulder.

Placing this hand too far to the left on the handle creates a *weak* grip, generally resulting in loss of distance, and contributing to a sliced shot.

A firm, but not tense grip (principally with the last three fingers of the left hand) promotes good club control, and prevents the fatal error of loosening the grip at the top of the backswing. Also, it is well to recess the grip of the left hand on the handle approximately one, or 1½ inches from the end. This will aid in preventing the grip from loosening at the top of the backswing, and further promote good club control and direction of the ball's flight.

In addition, when playing iron shots from the fairway, where a divot must be taken, a firm grip with the left hand reduces the chance of the club face opening up with the shock of impact. Should this happen, a definite sliced shot would result.

ITEM 2. While the illustrating photo seems to exaggerate the placing of the right hand against the club handle, this is done to stress the importance of keeping the palm of the right hand facing the target during the initial gripping of the club with the right hand when addressing the ball, and at the point of impact with the ball in the downswing.

Actually, when the *right*-hand grip is completed, this hand is placed slightly under the club handle, with the right arm relaxed. No finger knuckles of this hand should be seen by the player. Also, *under no circumstances* should the thumb be placed straight down on *top* of the handle.

ITEM 3. The right thumb should be placed firmly *across* the shaft handle to the *upper left side,* and with pressure of the first thumb joint applied to the handle. The forefinger should be *slightly* extended (like pulling the trigger of a pistol), and crooked around the handle with pressure applied by the second joint of this finger. The handle is therefore cradled across this finger, which should now be allowed to touch the end of the thumb.

A great deal of the control in the grip of the right hand is provided by the pressure of the thumb and first two fingers. There are some golfers who have the habit of extending the right forefinger slightly crooked and *loose* against the right side of the shaft handle (a professional never does this). To follow this practice reduces the control of the club during the swing, and at impact with the ball. A loss of distance in the shot, as well as control of the ball's flight direction is often the natural result.

ITEM 4. In completing the right-hand grip, the *left* thumb is snugly fitted into the heel of the palm of the right hand, with pressure of the fleshy base of the right thumb against the left thumb to be maintained throughout the entire swing. The more closely together the two hands are placed, the better the control of the club throughout.

Finally, assuming the most popular grip is used, the (Vardon) overlap, place the *little* finger of the right hand over the *forefinger* of the left hand. The "V" between the thumb and forefinger of both hands should now point toward the right shoulder.

NOTE:

The *interlocking* grip is formed by entwining the little finger of the right hand *between* the first and second fingers of the left hand.

The *baseball* grip places *all* fingers of both hands on the club handle.

We suggest that you see your school instructor or PGA teaching professional for advice on the proper grip for you, before you become too accustomed to one which may not be suitable for your particular needs. It is sometimes difficult to change.

NOW!

You should be able to properly grip your clubs. All necessary elements of the grip have been outlined in detail, illustrated, and explained.

The rest is *up to you*.

Practice your grip, both with and without swinging your clubs, until you automatically grip them the same way every time you use them (except for necessary adjustments for intentional hook or fade shots etc., explained later in this manual).

## THE STANCE

The square stance is recommended for most golfers.

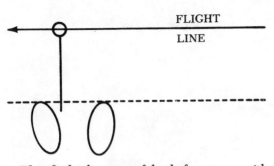

FLIGHT LINE

This finds the toes of both feet *even* with an imaginary line parallel to the flight line.

The open stance is used when playing an intentional fade or sliced shot.

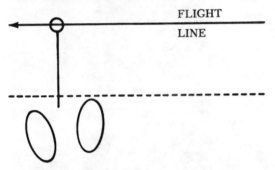

FLIGHT LINE

It is also used when the shorter irons are played, since there is less body turn, and a more upright swing arc.

The closed stance is used when playing an intentional hook or draw shot, from *right* to *left*.

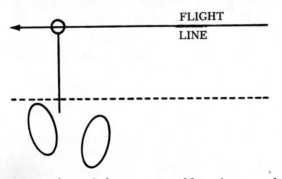

FLIGHT LINE

It is also a help to some older players, who find it difficult to get sufficient body turn in the backswing.

NOTE: *Before* positioning the feet, place the club head behind the ball, *square* to the intended flight line, with the sole of the club head *flat* on the ground. *Then* position the feet.

## THE TEE SHOT

### The Same Way—Every Time

The authors refer to this part of the instruction for the swing as the "basic" swing, because it covers the fundamental procedures so necessary, or essential to proper performance in the tee shot on a *consistent* basis.

Quite likely, many of us have noticed that certain amateur players seem to be able to consistently "keep their ball in play." Their golf shots off the tee, or on the fairway, seem to always be "down the middle," and straight for the target or objective point.

Why is this?

We believe it is because such players have firmly fixed in their minds the *techniques* which *must be considered in every shot,* and the proper *sequence* in which these things should be employed.

The next and most important factor in their success is that each time they address their ball, they make sure that everything pertinent to that particular shot has been carefully considered, and as a result, they do the *same things* the *same way every time.*

We fully recognize the variations in the manner in which certain golf shots must be executed, in cases where hazards must be overcome, or when playing certain of the shorter irons.

This does not apply to the tee shot, however, where the execution should always be the same, except for adjustments necessary under certain windy conditions, etc.

In the following pages, a 'step-by-step chronology of the techniques for the tee shot is outlined. Make up your mind that you are going to learn them. Not the words necessarily, but the techniques themselves—and the proper sequence in the execution. Then, every time that you step up to the teeing area to make your drive, check in your mind quickly, *what* you are supposed to do, and *do it*. Once this review has been accomplished, forget it, and go ahead and hit!

## What to Do

### STEP 1. STANCE AND ADDRESS

1. Tee ball (with one-half of ball above club head when it is grounded).

2. Step back and line up target from behind ball.

3. Grip club, as indicated on preceding pages. Grip with left hand first.

4. Place club head behind ball with sole *flat* on ground, and club face square to target. Right-hand grip to be completed after taking proper stance.

5. Take stance as follows:

    A. Ball positioned opposite *instep* of *left foot*.

    B. Left shoulder pointing toward target.

    C. Weight equally on heels and soles of feet. Right foot pointed slightly to right for fuller turn on backswing.

    D. Left toe pointed out more than right foot to provide good balance on downswing.

    E. Feet spread approximately the width of shoulders.

    F. Flex knees—"sit down to the ball," but *don't crouch!*

    G. Bend upper body forward *slightly*, approximately thirty degrees.

    H. Left hand, arm, and club shaft should form a line straight from club head to left shoulder. The hands will then be just inside of the left thigh and slightly ahead of the ball.

    I. Arch wrists slightly, particularly the right. *Don't reach for the ball.*

## How to Do It

To provide the most natural and comfortable position at address, the weight must be *equally* divided between both feet.

Also, highly important, the pressure must be on the *inside* of the feet, where it should remain throughout the swing.

Position the ball opposite the *instep* of the left foot, except when hitting into a headwind, in which case the ball is played more to the right.

Left arm, hand, and club shaft form a straight line from club head to the left shoulder.

This assures a high trajectory, which provides greater carrying distance in the ball's flight than one teed and hit low.

If the downswing is right, the ball will not be "blooped" high, and for only a short distance. However, when hitting into a headwind, the ball should be teed lower, and played more toward the center of the stance.

ITEM 2. After teeing the ball, it is well to step back facing the intended flight direction, to determine where you want the ball to land, considering such things as wind direction, fairway hazards, ground slopes, etc. Then take your stance as outlined, under Item 5B on page 24.

ITEM 3. Gripping the club with the left hand only, at first, enables the player to square the club face to the target, and to have the shaft in a straight line with the left arm and shoulder.

ITEM 4. Placing the club head behind the ball, square to the intended line of flight, before taking your stance, helps to assure a straight hit. It also determines how far from the ball the stance should be. *Don't reach* for the ball so that the club head is resting only on its heel. When proper stance position is completed, the hips, shoulders, and club face must be square to the target. Then complete the grip with the right hand without turning the body laterally. Should such a turn occur, the right-hand placement on the club handle might pull the right side of the body out, changing the squareness of alignment. This could cause a hit from the outside in, resulting in either a sharply pulled shot or a slice.

The weight is neither forward, nor back, but should be evenly divided between the *sole* and the *heel* of each foot.

Flex the knees—"sit down to the ball," and bend the upper body forward about thirty degrees.

Arch the wrists slightly (particularly the right) to assure not being too close to the ball, and to make certain that the sole of the club head is *flat* on the ground. *Don't reach for the ball.*

ITEM 5A. Positioning the ball opposite the instep of the left foot (assuming the rest of the stance is correct) assures hitting slightly on the upswing just *after* the bottom of the downswing arc has been reached. The result is a clean, solid hit for good distance, through a high trajectory of the ball's flight.

## Why You Do It

ITEM 1. Teeing the ball as described under this item enables the player to hit the ball slightly on the *upswing* at impact, near the *top* of the club face, assuming the ball is positioned correctly, opposite the left instep.

ITEM 5B. With the left shoulder pointing toward the target, the stance should be *square* to the direction line desired. A closed stance (left foot slightly ahead of the right) induces a hooked shot, while an open stance (right foot slightly ahead of the left), contributes to more of a fade, or a slice. It is acknowledged, however, that there are times when either a closed or an open stance should be used, particularly when playing an intentional hook or fade shot. This is covered in the section "Professional Tips."

Also, some players prefer to use either a slightly closed or slightly open stance for their tee shots, either of which may be better adapted to the individual's personal style of swing. This is often due to certain characteristics such as age, swing arc, physical deficiencies, etc. In general, however, the square stance produces the best results for most people.

ITEM 5C. When the weight is distributed equally on the heels, as well as the soles of both feet at address, good balance in the entire swing is more easily attained. There should be a feeling of slight pressure on the insteps, but not to the extent that the body is thrown forward toward the ball in the downswing.

ITEMS 5C and D. Pointing the right foot slightly to the right, and the left foot out a little more to the left, helps to unblock the hips in both the backswing and the downswing. This allows a fuller turn in the backswing, and a smooth downswing with a full follow-through without loss of balance.

ITEM 5E. For all wood shots as well as the long irons, the feet at address should be spread approximately the width of the shoulders. When the spread is less than this, the full power of the swing is lost, and the swing arc is restricted. When the spread is too wide, proper turning of the hips and shoulders is prevented in both the backswing and the downswing, again reducing the swing arc, and flattening the entire swing.

As the shorter clubs are used, the spread of the feet narrows, because less power is required, and the swing arc is shorter and more upright.

ITEMS 5F and G. Flexing the knees, "sitting down to the ball," assures a firm but relaxed stance at address, putting the body in position to pivot properly without swaying. *Don't crouch!* When accompanied with the shoulders slumped forward slightly, the head is pulled down, and the upper body is bent forward approximately thirty degrees. This entire body position now permits addressing the club to the ball at the proper angle and distance.

ITEM 5H. Keeping the left hand, arm, and club shaft in a straight line from the club head to the left shoulder, places the hands slightly *ahead* of the ball at address as they should be for all golf shots. This allows the hands, arms, and club to start the backswing in a firm, controlled motion, preventing an early wrist break, which causes the club head to be picked up sharply.

Since the position of the left arm, hands, and club head at impact is usually the same as at address, this again places the hands ahead of the ball to lead the club head through and out toward the target.

ITEM 5I. Arching the wrists slightly (particularly the right) prevents the hands from being too close to the body at address, which might result in picking up the club head on the backswing. It also assures that the sole of the club head will be flat on the ground at address.

In addition, when the stance is finally completed, make sure that the *right* shoulder is lower than the left at address. However, it should *not* be extended forward across the intended flight line, because this would spoil the squareness of the stance alignment. (Additional coverage of shoulder positions during the *swing* will be found in following pages.)

## What to Do

### STEP 2. THE BACKSWING

1. Waggle club head (*reduces tension*).

2. Set club head behind ball.

3. Cock head to right, and make slight forward press to left with hands and right knee.

4. Start backswing (*low* and *slow*) with a push from left side through left hand and arm. Club head should be dragged away from ball with left arm and club shaft forming a straight line, and with club head kept low to ground for first twelve to twenty-four inches. At same time:

A. Turn hips to right until back faces target (*don't sway hips laterally*).

B. Left shoulder turns to right until it drops under chin.

C. Left knee dips in to right.

D. Weight shifts to right foot, with pressure on *inside* of foot.

5. Keep arms *fully extended,* with left arm in line with club shaft.

6. Keep both arms straight, and don't break wrists until hands are at least hip high.

7. Continue backswing until hands reach shoulder height or higher, depending on player's ability. *Don't bend left arm.*

8. *Keep head still* and *eye on ball.*

9. At top of backswing, *don't loosen grip on club.*

10. Keep backswing well within your physical limits. *Don't stretch or strain.*

11. When top of backswing is reached, start downswing automatically, start unwinding.

## How to Do It

Start backswing, *low* and *slow,* with *both* arms *fully* extended. Don't pick up club head sharply from the ground. Keep it low to ground for *first twelve to twenty-four inches.*

The backswing turn. Swivel the hips to the right (don't sway laterally).

*Don't loosen grip on club* at top of backswing
(note position of right hand on grip).

Top of backswing. Note full shoulder turn, with left arm comfortably straight, and club head pointing toward target.

## Why You Do It

ITEM 1. Waggling the club head before the start of the backswing is a combination of slight wrist, arm, and club movement to relieve tension. It also helps to start the backswing in a smooth manner.

ITEM 2. Setting the club head behind the ball again, just before starting the backswing, places it in the same position as at the initial address, for the correct start of club movement.

ITEM 3. Cocking the head to the right just before the start of the backswing, like the forward press, helps to start the backswing in motion. It gets the head and chin out of the way, permitting the tilt and turn of the left shoulder. This also helps the body to take a longer, less inhibited turn than if the head were straight forward. In addition, it helps to prevent swaying to the left and beyond the ball at impact, in the downswing.

The forward press is a slight movement of the hands, body, and right knee to the left, setting the swing in motion as a recoil from this movement. This also relieves tension since it is a continuation of the waggle.

The start of the backswing finds the right knee still bent slightly toward the ball, putting the weight automatically on the inside of the right foot.

ITEM 4. Starting the backswing *low* and *slow,* with the club head close to the ground for the first twelve to twenty-four inches, and with left arm, hand, and club shaft in a straight line, prevents picking up the club head through a collapse of the straight left arm. This results in throwing the club head over the right shoulder, and tends to sway the body laterally to the right.

ITEM 4A. The hips will automatically turn toward the right if the backswing is started as described above, provided the head is kept still, and no lateral sway to the right takes place.

ITEM 4B. When the left shoulder is pulled around to the right, it lowers until it drops under the chin, while the right shoulder raises.

At all times during the backswing, the upper body and the head *must* stay over the ball. (The correct position is like having a rod running through the body from top to bottom vertically, and the body pivoting around this rod.) The upper body is now coiled for a strong uncoiling action to be started by the downswing.

ITEM 4C. Dipping the left knee in to the right naturally accompanies the body pivot action, placing the left foot in position for the weight to be shifted to the inside of this foot on the downswing. *Guard against lifting the heel off the ground too far.* This could cause excessive body sway to the right in the backswing.

ITEM 4D. The weight shift to the inside of the right foot takes place naturally during the backswing pivot. It is, however, not a true weight shift, but actually a bracing of the right foot during the pivot process. Most of the weight rests on the ball of the left foot at this point. What happens is a straightening of the right knee (but not locking it), with the pivot creating a coiling action around this leg. When this coiling is released in the downswing, the right knee is thrust toward the target, providing much of the power for the hit.

ITEMS 5 and 6. Keeping both arms fully extended to the point where the hands reach hip level approximately, prevents picking up the club head sharply as described in Item 4. When this point is reached, the right elbow starts to bend in close to the right side of the body. The wrist break or cocking action should take place naturally as the hands are raised above this level.

ITEM 7. The higher the player's hands are brought in the full backswing, the greater the swing arc, and resulting distance to be attained in the hit. However, this height must be adjusted according to the individual player's ability. Older players particularly sometimes find that their shoulder muscles are not supple enough to permit a full backswing. Generally the difference in distance to be attained between a three-quarter swing and a full backswing is only about fifteen to twenty yards for most players.

ITEM 8. Keeping the head and body still during the backswing prevents lateral sway, and moving away from the target. There is bound to be some movement, and the way to keep it at a minimum is to twist the body in the pivot, instead of swaying laterally. When the body and head moves, it is also difficult to keep the eye on the ball. The result is a scuffed or topped shot.

ITEM 9. Loosening the grip at the top of the backswing creates "floating hands." The position of the club head generally is changed from what it was at address, and it is difficult, if not impossible, to regrip and correct the club head alignment in the downswing. When this occurs, anything can happen except a solid, clean hit at impact with the ball.

Keep pressure with the last three fingers of the left hand (particularly the little finger) on the club handle throughout the entire swing.

ITEM 10. Don't try to stretch the backswing beyond the point of your individual ability. Again, assuming the rest of your swing is good, the difference in distance through either a full or three-quarter backswing is negligible, particularly when the player with the shorter swing develops accuracy with his drives, and fairway wood and iron shots.

ITEM 11. During the entire backswing process, the upper body has been coiled for release with the power in the downswing. The start of the downswing automatically becomes the beginning of this uncoiling.

## What to Do

### STEP 3. THE DOWNSWING

1. Start downswing slowly. Don't turn body to left too quickly. *Don't be too eager to hit.*
2. Delay complete turn of body toward target, to allow hands and arms to come through.
3. Lead club down with left hand and arm. "Draw" arms down with left arm kept straight (until completely through impact with ball).
4. Delay uncocking of wrists until hands reach *hip level* approximately.
5. Weight shifts to left foot. Move *hips* first,

then shoulders, to left, then arms and hands. Thrust *right* knee to left—*push off inside* of right foot.
6. *Right* elbow returns to side *slightly in front of body.*
7. Now uncock wrists, snapping them into a straight line with the arms, bringing the club head into the ball at the right time.
8. *Right* shoulder lowers naturally (down and under) until it touches chin.
9. *Keep head still, and eye on ball.*

NOTE:

Keep your swing *smooth* and *rhythmic.*
Don't try to "*slug*" beyond your power.
Good timing will often get more distance for you than a "slugged" shot.

## How to Do It

"*Pull*" arms and hands down hard toward the ball (mostly with the *left* arm). *Don't be too eager to hit.*

*Hips* lead the downswing. Next, the shoulders, then the hands and arms.

Right elbow returns to side, slightly in front of the body, with wrists still cocked.

Thrust right knee to left, and push off with *inside* of right foot.

## Why You Do It

ITEM 1. The speed of the backswing and the downswing should be relatively the same, as long as the entire swing is smooth. This is called timing. For some players, the swing will be faster than for others, and you must determine the cadence best suited to your style and ability. In essence, a little faster swing helps to promote a harder hit, but the player should never press or allow a jerky motion to creep in.

Swinging the shoulders around to the left too quickly could throw the club head out across the flight line, and the hands away from the body. This could cause a badly pulled shot or a slice, or even a half-topped impact.

The proper start of the downswing begins with the *hips* rotating to the left quickly, followed by the turn of the shoulders to the left. This causes the hands and arms to move. (Hips make a slight lateral slide to the left before rotating.)

ITEMS 2 and 3. While the upper body must turn as described above, a premature complete turn causes "hitting from the top" with resulting loss of power.

Lead the club down with a strong pull of the left hand, with the top of the club handle pointing toward the ground, and the wrists *still cocked.*

ITEMS 4, 5, and 6. Uncocking of the wrists too soon would lose much of the desired club-head speed. When the hips move first, then the shoulders, then the hands and arms, as described in Item 3, the right elbow returns to the right side of the body, as indicated in the photo illustrations. The wrists are still cocked at this point. When the right knee is thrust forward toward the target, just before uncocking the wrists, and with a *push off* the inside of the right foot, the club head is put into a strong hitting position, which releases the right side to follow the hit.

ITEMS 7 and 8. With the uncocking of the wrists, a split second before impact with the ball, the club-head speed is increased to the maximum at the point of impact, through the release or uncocking of wrists being completed at the exact bottom of the downswing. This snaps them through the ball, with the right hand passing the left in the process. Maximum distance in the hit is the natural result.

ITEM 9. Once again, keeping the head as still as possible, and the eye on the ball, prevents lunging or lateral sway to the left in the downswing, which could ruin the hit. If your entire swing has been correct, you won't need to look up to see where the ball is going. It will go straight and true, where you intended—and LONG!

## What to Do

### STEP 4. IMPACT AND FOLLOW-THROUGH

1. Just before impact with the ball, make sure that *right* shoulder comes down and under the chin. This shoulder moves farther to left than its position at address. *Left* shoulder rises.

2. At impact, the left arm is kept straight, and right arm is slightly bent.

3. Hit "through" the ball, and not *at it. Don't quit on the shot.*

4. After impact, extend arms as far as possible —with follow-through *low,* and weight shifted to *inside* of left foot at first.

5. Finish follow-through on *outside* of left foot, with body turned toward target. At this point, *weight must be on left foot,* with *right* foot on *toe,* merely steadying the body, and right knee pointing toward target. *Don't finish with weight on right foot.*

(Don't "flip" the club head at the target.)

*Keep eye on ball until well after impact.*

## How to Do It

*Hit through the ball—not at it.*
Follow through low and completely. "Throw" the club head at the target.

Extend both arms as far as possible. Shift weight fully to the left side. Keep eye on ball until *well after impact*.

Finish follow-through with hands high, and weight completely on left leg.

Right knee faces target, with toe of right foot balancing body.

*Now*, look up to see where the ball is going. *Don't look up before this.*

## Why You Do It

ITEM 1. As a preliminary to actual impact with the ball, one must be sure that the *right* shoulder comes down and under the chin just before the impact.

Actually, this shoulder at impact moves farther to the left than its original position at address. This assures that the body weight has properly shifted to the left, and that the *left* shoulder continues to rise throughout the impact and into the follow-through. This smooth forward and upward rise of the left shoulder automatically brings the right shoulder down and under as described above.

ITEM 2. During the actual impact, the left arm is *straight* to assure firmness in the hit, and to maintain good club-head control. However, the *right* arm must be slightly *bent*. Should the right arm be straight at impact, power in the hit will be spent too rapidly.

The key to power in the hit, as well as accuracy, is the delayed wrist action, or uncocking of the wrists in the downswing, just before impact with the ball. This generally results from keeping the right elbow close to the body, and bringing the right shoulder down and under as the club head whips through at the ball.

The left hand must be the controlling and guiding element of the swing. If this hand is maintaining this control, however, one may hit as hard as possible with the right hand, provided it does not overpower the left. Should this happen, it is generally because the left hand is not keeping the proper control. ——

ITEM 3. After the impact, the right arm must immediately straighten in order to provide maximum acceleration of the club head.

The most important thing a player should have fixed in his mind on *all full shots* with every club, is to make certain that he hits "through" the ball *fully*, rather than just *at* the ball. A smooth, full swing through the hitting area, "throwing" the club head at the target, will help to promote accuracy and provide good distance in the shot.

This enables the ball to "ride" on the club face for a split second longer after the natural compression of the ball at impact, and the resulting recoil of compression after the hit. This is in sharp contrast to the ineffectual results of simply slapping at the ball and quitting on the follow-through. Don't try to steer the ball, and don't just flip the club head at the target.

ITEMS 4 and 5. Following through *low,* and with fully extended arms, will make it certain that the player has hit "through" the ball, and has shifted the weight to the left foot. Adequate body turn toward the target at the finish of the follow-through brings both hips around to a point at right angles to the target. The weight must then rest mainly on the left foot, with the body being steadied by the toe of the right foot. The body will then be facing forward, and the right knee will also be pointing toward the target.

The head must be held behind the ball, and as motionless as possible, throughout the downswing and the impact, and the eyes on the ball position until well after impact. As the follow-through takes place, and the body is forced around in a position facing the target, the head should turn slowly to the target as a result of the body turn. Don't be a "peeker" and look up too soon. There is plenty of time to see the ball's flight after the hit.

## THERE YOU HAVE IT!

The four steps of the basic swing, completely outlined, illustrated, and explained.

There is nothing difficult about it, once you have *memorized* the techniques in each step, and *practiced* them until your mind and body become accustomed to doing *automatically* what each step calls for.

Practice each step separately at first, then the complete swing.

*Now* see a competent golf instructor and arrange for a *series* of private lessons in your swing execution, until your instructor is satisfied that you have developed a sound, strong, and smooth swing.

You can usually get a lower rate for a series of lessons, and you will probably need them. Very few students are successful in accomplishing their purpose with just one lesson.

Remember, the game of golf cannot be

learned from books alone. We hope, however, that this book will help you to understand what your teacher is telling and showing you, and to keep you on the beam when he is not available during your practice sessions.

The whole purpose of this book is to outline the execution techniques in such a simple and concise manner that *anyone* willing to study and *memorize* them can progress faster than through any other method we know of.

We urge you to try it! And we think you will be amazed at the results.

*Good luck!*

## GOLF TERMS AND GOLF ETIQUETTE

Now that you have learned to swing a golf club satisfactorily, you are ready to play some good practice rounds with your good friends.

Many of those with whom you will play have been playing the game for a number of years and are familiar with golf terms and golf etiquette.

To acquaint you with these features and save possible embarrassment, we believe these points should closely follow your initial instruction.

We suggest that you purchase a copy of the latest United States Golf Association Rules. They may be obtained at your golf course pro shop at a nominal cost—about twenty-five cents.

The more you follow the rules of golf play, and of golf etiquette, the more certain you will become a desirable playing companion.

One of the most flagrant violations of good etiquette is the *failure to replace divots*, both in the fairway and on the green. Good players *always* do, and you can win the respect of your playing companions and help to keep your favorite golf course in better shape if you not only replace your own divots, but also those overlooked by less thoughtful players.

There are many ways in life that one can become known as a thoroughbred, and this is one of them.

## GLOSSARY OF GOLF TERMS

Since this book is primarily for the beginner, the following glossary of golf terms is not all-inclusive. It contains only those with which the newcomer to golfdom should be familiar.

ADDRESS   Position taken by a player in preparing to start a stroke.

BIRDIE   Score for a hole played in one stroke *under* par.

BOGEY   Score for a hole played in one stroke *over* par.

CLUB FACE   Striking surface of the club head.

DIVOT   Sod cut with club head after striking ball.

EAGLE   A score for a hole played in two strokes *under* par.

FAIRWAY   The portion of terrain between the tee and green which is well kept to provide a favorable lie for the ball.

FORE   A warning to be made to another player that a ball is about to be, or has been, hit in his direction.

FOURSOME   Describes a four-ball match in which four players participate.

GREEN   The putting surface at the conclusion of each hole played.

HAZARD   Any bunker, water (except "casual water"), ditch, sand trap, or other obstruction between tee and green.

HEEL   The part of the club at which the shaft is fastened to the club head.

HOLE   Units of play from tee to green. A round consists of eighteen holes or units.

HONOR   The side or player having priority on the tee because of winning the previous hole.

HOOK   To hit ball in a curve to the left of the intended line of flight.

HOSEL   Hollow part of club-head socket into which shaft is fitted, at the neck of the club.

LOFT   Angle at which club face is set from vertical. Influences the extent in which the ball can be lifted in flight for various clubs.

OUT-OF-BOUNDS   Ground on which play is prohibited.

PAR   Standard score for a hole.

PENALTY STROKE   A stroke added to the score of a side, or individual player, under certain rules.

PROVISIONAL BALL   A ball played after previous ball "probably" has gone out of bounds, has been lost, or is believed unplayable.

PULL   To hit the ball straight, but to the left of the intended line of flight.

PUSH   To hit the ball straight, but to the right of the intended line. This differs from the slice, which curves to the right.

PUTT   Playing a stroke on the green.

ROUGH   Heavy long grass fringing fairway or green.

SHANK   To hit the ball with the socket or neck (hosel) of the club.

SLICE   A clockwise spin which causes ball to curve to right of intended line of flight.

SOLE   Bottom of club head.

STANCE   Position of feet at address or while stroking club.

TEEING GROUND  Often called the tee. Starting place for the hole to be played. Indicated in front by two markers.

TOE  Forward part of club head.

TOP  To strike ball above center.

WAGGLE  Preliminary action of flexing wrists, causing club to swing forward and backward.

## GOLF ETIQUETTE

1. No one should move or talk, or stand close to, or directly behind, the ball or hole when a player is making a stroke.
2. The player who has the honor should be allowed to play before his opponent tees his ball.
3. No player should play until the party in front is out of range.
4. When play has been completed, players should immediately leave the putting green.
5. Players while looking for a lost ball should allow other players coming up to pass them. They should signal such players to pass, and having given such signal, should not continue to play until the passing players are out of range.
6. A player should replace and press down all divots cut by him. Also, he should repair ball marks on the green.
7. Players should carefully fill or smooth all holes or footmarks made by them in sand traps.
8. Players should see that neither they nor their caddies injure the surface of the green by standing close to the hole when the ground is soft, or in replacing the flag stick.
9. A player who has incurred a penalty should indicate this to his opponent as soon as possible.
10. Players should play without undue delay at all times.
11. Players whose balls have reached the green should not leave their carts or golf bags at the front approach to the green. Such equipment should be moved to the side or rear of the green after ball has landed on this surface. To leave equipment in front delays following players unnecessarily, and creates the chance of being hit by their approach shots.
12. A player should not walk in front or ahead of others in his group who have not completed their shots. This is not only dangerous, but disturbing to those about to make their strokes.

*Be a good sport!* Compliment your opponent when he makes a good shot. A little praise never hurt anybody—even *you.*

# SECTION TWO

# THE FAIRWAY WOODS

For the Nos. 2, 3, and 4 woods, a simple chronology of the techniques is outlined under the heading of "What to Do." We urge you to study and memorize these techniques. The illustrations show how to do it, and subsequent pages answer your possible questions as to why you do it.

If you love the game as most golfers do, the study and practice of the techniques will definitely prove worth your efforts. You will be surprised at the short time it takes to learn to make good clean shots from the fairway with your woods.

Before getting into the subject of your fairway woods shots, we suggest that you pay close attention to this chapter and read about what frequently happens to the player who takes no pregame warmup.

If you have any doubts, see your PGA teaching professional.

## THIS GAME OF GOLF

### The Pregame Warmup

How often has the average golfer stepped up to the first tee feeling that "this is his day," the day he is going to have one of his best rounds?

It is a beautiful day, with little or no wind. The other members of the foursome are fine companions, and a good competitive match has been arranged.

His drive is fairly good—not long, but straight down the fairway. As he strolls toward his ball, he is convinced that today he "really has it." Then something happens!

He has probably started out "cold," with no practice warmup. His body muscles are not yet tuned to the work they are being required to do, and what is perhaps worse, his superconfidence (while a good attitude) is far out of proportion to the equally important requirement, *concentration*.

He forgets to concentrate on his second shot, and as a result it ends up only a few yards from where it was hit. Frustrated, he tries again thinking more about the preceding poor shot than what he must do to recover, and the same thing happens again.

Now he begins to press, embarrassed because he feels he is letting his partners down, and you know the rest—he finishes the first hole with a triple bogey or worse. While there may be some improvement on the next two holes, his total score for the first three eliminates all chance of a good first round of nine holes.

Why let this happen, or at least why not try to prevent it by taking a good warmup before starting? Swinging a club for a while before starting will help, but fifteen to thirty minutes on the practice range is the real solution. In this amount of time the body muscles have loosened, the need for concentration has been established, and you are ready.

Come out to the course a little ahead of your game time, use your practice range often —then watch your game improve.

## THE FAIRWAY WOODS

You now have some idea of the necessity and scoring importance of pregame warmup, and the continuing value of *concentrating* on every shot played throughout a round of golf.

The all-important first three holes are those in which a good start is made, or they can become the nemesis to a good-scoring round.

So, too, can the last three holes. These come at a time when you are beginning to tire, particularly those who do not play often. The legs are tired, shoulders and muscles are getting stiff, and you begin to feel just a little older. So you begin to try harder and press, which can only result in overswinging, and getting off balance. Result, you miss some of your shots—most of them—and up goes your score for the second nine holes.

When this happens, it is better to make your swing more compact, with a shorter backswing, and settle for a little less distance if necessary. With an easier swing and concentration on your remaining shots, the last three holes should not spoil your game.

Since the matter of obtaining distance in most of your fairway shots is an important part of good scoring, the use of fairway woods is essential for the average golfer. On all par five holes, as well as most of the par four holes, a fairway wood of some kind is the required club to use if you expect to hit the green in the regulation number of strokes.

These woods are the *distance* clubs, and are called for when maximum distance is required, and the lie of the ball or the elements does not force you to consider an iron instead.

For many golfers, particularly newcomers, using a fairway wood presents many problems, but this really does not need to be so. It is true that it is much easier to hit a ball that is teed up than one which lies close to the ground, or which might even be somewhat buried in the turf or in a divot mark.

This section is devoted to the use of various types of fairway woods, and how they may be played to get the best results. When you learn to use them properly, you will soon gain the necessary confidence, and shots off the fairway will cease to worry you.

Once again, the first thing to do is to see your PGA teaching professional. He is the one to get you started right in using the subject of this section—the fairway woods.

## HIT HARD FOR DISTANCE

Before getting into the subject of which of the fairway woods to use, and how to use them, there are several most important points to keep in mind:

1. Correct ball position.
2. Swing smoothly, and keep your balance. Keep eye on the ball.
3. Hit *hard,* but don't *lunge.*
4. Follow through *completely.*

This photo of the illustrator, Dale Mead, shows the perfect follow-through and body position at the finish of the swing. With this kind of finish, there can be no doubt that the player has hit *through* the ball, and not just *at* it. This is the secret for straight, long hits with the fairway woods.

## NO. 2 WOOD

### What to Do

1. As for all shots, size up your lie and the objectives as you approach your ball.

2. Select the No. 2 wood *only* if the ball is *sitting up well* and can be cleanly hit.

3. Take your stance almost the same as for normal tee shots, but with the ball positioned off the *left heel*. Make sure the sole of the club head is flat on the ground at address, and *square to the target*.

4. Use the same basic swing as for the drive off the tee, except that the ball should be hit at the *bottom* of the downswing.

5. The object is to "sweep" the ball off the turf with only a slight scarring of the grass. Don't lunge at the ball.

6. Trying to punch down on the ball that is in a good lie may often result in a shot "blooped" high in the air.

7. Keep the *head still* and your *eye on the ball* until well after the hit has been completed.

8. Avoid the urge to look up too quickly to see if the ball is well hit and on its way. It only takes a *fraction of a second* to lose your concentration and end up with a topped shot.

9. Follow through *low*, with *fully extended arms*, and with weight finishing on *left foot* the same as for all full shots.

10. Keep your swing smooth, and in one piece.

### How to Do It

Address and ball position.

*Sweep* club back—with *fully extended arms.*

Top of backswing—with full shoulder turn,     and club head pointing toward target.

Follow through with fully extended arms.     Let right side of body follow the swing.

Finish swing with hands high—body facing    target, and weight on *left* foot.

## Why You Do It

ITEM 1. Having made your tee shot, you will be approaching the spot where your ball has landed (we hope in the fairway). Use this time to determine things such as wind direction and intervening hazards, and what club to use. This latter decision can be finally made after you have reached the ball and inspected the lie. The main thing is that at this point you now have only one thing to think about—what club to use, and the execution of a good shot.

ITEM 2. Because the club face loft of the No. 2 wood is less than that of a No. 3 wood, unless you have an *excellent lie* in the fairway, use the 3 wood instead, to assure getting the ball off the ground with a good clean hit. Many professionals do not even carry a 2 wood in their bag. The difference in distance to be attained between the two clubs is negligible.

ITEM 3. For *level* lies, the stance is similar to that of the tee shot, except that the ball is positioned off the *left heel,* instead of the left instep. (This is assuming that one is not hitting into a headwind, in which case the ball is positioned farther back toward the center of the stance.)

ITEMS 4 and 5. The ball being positioned opposite the left heel allows it to be hit at the exact *bottom* of the swing arc. No divot should be taken in this shot, as the ball is "swept" off the ground, and the grass merely scarred.

ITEM 6. Unlike most iron shots, one does not hit down with the wood clubs in quite the same manner. (You do hit down with wood clubs to some degree, particularly when the ball is buried in heavy clover or lies in a divot.) You must never try to hit the ball on the upswing either, however, or try to scoop the ball up—only a topped or scuffed shot can result.

ITEMS 7 and 8. As in the case of all golf shots, keeping the head still prevents body sway and resulting "fat" hits, scuffed shots, topped hits. Of equal importance is the matter of keeping the eye on the ball *until well after it is hit.* If

your swing is correct and well-timed, you won't have to raise your head prematurely to see where the ball is going. It will go where you want it most of the time if you have executed your shot properly.

ITEM 9. The follow-through for fairway shots is the same as for tee shots, *low* and *complete,* with the hands finishing high. This should assure a straight shot for good distance, assuming other factors of the address and swing have been executed properly.

ITEM 10. Keeping your swing smooth and compact will promote good timing. Lunging at the ball in an effort to gain more distance will quite likely work just in reverse—resulting in a missed shot. A "one-piece" swing with good timing usually provides more distance than when one tries to "kill" the ball.

## NO. 3 WOOD

### What to Do

1. Line up your next shot as you approach your ball.
2. If your ball is sitting down in the grass, or if you have any doubt that it can be hit cleanly, use the No. 3 wood.
3. Many professionals do not even carry a No. 2 wood in their bag. The average distance difference is only about ten to fifteen yards.
4. Since the shaft is shorter for the No. 3 wood than for Nos. 1 and 2 woods, stand slightly closer to the ball.
5. For the No. 3 wood, the ball should be played a few inches to the right of the left heel.
6. At address, the club head should be set *flat* on the ground in its natural lie, so as not to distort the loft of the club.
7. On the downswing, the club face is brought into the ball *before* it has reached the bottom of the swing arc. A turf divot will, therefore, be taken after the ball has been hit.
8. Don't try to "punch" down so hard that you end up with too large a divot, and no distance to your shot.
9. Use the same smooth and complete follow-through as for all full shots.

**How to Do It**

Keep arms fully extended, throughout—impact with ball, and in follow-through after impact.

To assure hitting ball *before* taking turf divot.

Allowing arms to bend causes scuffed shots and "bloopers."

Address—with ball positioned a few inches to right of left foot.

(To assure bringing club face into ball *before* reaching the bottom of the swing arc.)

NOTE: See illustrations shown for the No. 2 wood for other parts of the swing. Except for the slightly different ball position, the technique is the same.

## Why You Do It

ITEM 1. Once again, as you approach your ball after having made your tee shot, or for a par five hole, when you are hitting to the green, give consideration to the things necessary to attain your objective. Don't wait until you have reached your ball to start thinking of these things.

ITEMS 2 and 3. The No. 3 wood is the safest club to use in order to get the ball up and winging, and to attain the maximum distance possible. This is assuming a shorter and more lofted wood club is not the better choice, because of a following wind, or the distance to target being less than that which would require a longer wood club.

ITEM 4. Since the No. 3 wood shaft is shorter than Nos. 1 or 2 woods, the swing arc is therefore somewhat less. The player should stand closer to the ball for this shot, and the stance will be correct when addressing the ball, if the club head is resting *flat* on its sole. With the shorter shaft, the player will find himself a few inches closer to the ball than when using the longer woods.

ITEMS 5, 6, and 7. Playing the ball a few inches to the right of the left heel for the No. 3 wood shots (on a level lie) will bring the club head into the ball just *before* the bottom of the swing arc has been reached. The ball is hit first, with a divot taken after the impact.

ITEM 8. The player should guard against "punching" down so abruptly that he "bloops" the shot high and for only a short distance. Hitting the ball *before* the bottom of the swing arc has been reached is sufficient to create the condition of "hitting down" at the ball. It is not necessary to punch down excessively to assure getting the ball up in the air.

ITEM 9. For shots from a *level* lie, with a No. 3 wood, the player should not alter his swing from that of the longer wood clubs. The shorter shaft and shorter swing arc will take care of any difference. Of extreme importance is that the player should preserve his timing and keep his swing smooth and compact. Hit *through* the ball, and don't punch *at* it. Follow through completely, and finish the swing with the hands high.

## NO. 4 WOOD

### What to Do

1. Check your lie and intended course of action as you approach your ball.

2. The No. 4 wood is the club to use when good distance is required, and the following obstacles must be overcome:

   A. When the lie of the ball is buried deep in the turf.

   B. When the ball rests in fairly deep rough off the fairway, and is a good distance from the target.

   C. When the ball is sitting up well in a fairway bunker, and the forward lip of the bunker can be easily cleared. *Hit the ball cleanly.*

   D. When there is a tree in front of the line to the target, and a successful shot with a long iron is doubtful.

   E. On a downslope lie where extra loft is needed. Play the ball back toward the right foot.

3. Because of the shorter shaft, stand closer to the ball than for longer clubs. Make sure that the sole of the club head is *flat* on the ground at address.

4. Position the ball midway between the left heel and the center of stance for normal lies.

5. Use the same "one-piece" swing as for all full shots.

6. Keep the head still, and the eye on the ball throughout the complete swing.

7. Follow through *low* and *fully* as for all full swings. *Don't lunge at the ball or flip the club* in the follow-through.

8. Be sure to finish swing with the weight on the left foot.

**How to Do It**

Stand closer to ball for No. 4 wood, since the club shaft is shorter than the Nos. 2 or 3 woods.

Position ball at address—between *left* foot and center of stance.

Front view.

Playing out of deep rough, a long distance from target.

Use No. 4 wood—unless ball is buried in *tall* grass or weeds.

*Keep head still and eye on ball.*

Employ same techniques as shown for Nos. 2 or 3 woods for the complete swing.

Don't *lunge* at the ball, or try to chop it out.

Side view.

## Why You Do It

ITEM 1. Determining your course of action as you approach your ball for the next shot saves the necessity for filling your mind with these things after you take your stance. Besides, it speeds up play on the course.

One of the real great professional tournament players was asked how he could hit so quickly when he reached his ball. His answer was, "I have already figured out what I must do before I have reached my ball, and the fewer things I have to think about while preparing to execute my shot, the more *relaxed* and *positive* I can be, so I just go ahead and hit."

He further stated that "anyone who stands over his ball longer than *five seconds* is beginning to doubt himself."

Concentration is necessary, but the longer one

deliberates before making his shot, the more chance that the subconscious will become filled with disturbing elements which could make one too tense, and spoil the shot execution. So, once you have lined up your stance with the club you have decided to use, *go ahead and hit!*

ITEM 2A. When the ball is buried deep in the fairway turf, or in a deep divot, the No. 4 wood with its more lofted club face is the club to use. The loss of distance between this club and the longer fairway woods is negligible.

ITEM 2B. To use the No. 4 wood from fairly deep rough is all right provided the ball is not buried in very heavy grass or leafy weeds. For this condition, a more lofted short iron may be better, since the heavy growth may slow down the club head too much, or even divert its direction. With a slight adjustment in the swing, however, wherein the player hits down sharply at the ball (which is played more toward the *center* of the stance), one can nearly always attain more distance with a No. 4 wood than by using a long iron, much less a short one.

ITEM 2C. When good distance to the target is required, and the ball is "sitting up" well in a fairway bunker, the No. 4 wood is an excellent club to use, provided the forward lip of the bunker is low enough to be cleared. The ball *must be hit cleanly*, taking *no sand*. Don't ground the club head in the trap. It is against the rules.

ITEM 2D. When there is a tree in front of the line to the target, the extra loft of the No. 4 wood *usually* will clear the tree, provided the ball is far enough back from the tree to gain the height of flight necessary for clearance. When in doubt, use a long iron, and "punch" out to a safe position. Don't gamble and waste a stroke.

ITEM 2E. On a downslope lie, the club head should follow the contour of the slope. Therefore, to get the ball into the air safely, a more lofted club like the No. 4 wood is the desirable club to use. Playing the ball toward the *right* foot enables the club head to hit the ball at the proper point in the downswing.

ITEM 3. Using the No. 4 wood, stand even closer to the ball than for the No. 3 wood, because the shaft is a little shorter. The proper position of the stance is again determined by placing the sole of the club head *flat* on the ground, and with the stance and body position the same as for other wood clubs.

ITEMS 4 and 5. Positioning the ball midway between the left heel and the center of stance, for normal lies, assures that the ball will be hit *before* the bottom of the downswing arc has been reached. Make sure that the swing is smooth and compact, and that the club head is not punched down into the ground. The ball position will take care of the hit down into the ball.

ITEM 6. As for all shots, keep the *head still*, and the *eye on the ball* until well *after* the hit. Moving the head can cause a "fat" hit, and looking up can cause a topped shot.

ITEMS 7 and 8. A smooth, well-timed hit *through* the ball is essential for good distance. It is the same for all full shots. *Lunging* at the ball, or flipping the club head *at* it can never achieve the distance or straight flight to the target which is the desired objective. Again, finish the swing with the weight on the left foot, and the hands high.

### NOTE:

The foregoing pages have covered the use of the most popular and generally used wood clubs by most players, the Nos. 1, 2, 3, and 4 woods.

There are even more lofted wood clubs than these that many players find of real value in reaching their objectives, particularly women. See the comments in the next column concerning the No. 5 wood, and then check with your professional adviser whether some of these clubs might help *your* game.

## NO. 5 WOOD

Some golfers like to use a No. 5 wood occasionally, and some carry woods with even more loft.

These clubs have a certain value under extreme conditions, particularly when playing a shot out of very heavy rough where more distance is needed than can be expected from a very short iron.

Very few professionals use such clubs in tournament play, since they are restricted to a total of fourteen clubs in their bag at one time, and since they are experts.

To carry them would force the elimination of at least one of the longer woods, as well as one or more of the irons, which are generally put into play far more often.

There is a definite place for such clubs, however, particularly for our lady golfer, whose iron shots may not give her the distance she feels she can obtain from the higher lofted woods.

We strongly recommend the No. 5 wood for women golfers. Also we definitely recommend that golfers who have an average score of ninety or over discard the No. 2 wood and replace it with a No. 5 wood.

Your pro shop has them, and your professional instructor will be glad to advise you on this subject. He will also be glad to instruct you on the use of the No. 5 wood and others of even higher loft, if he feels they will materially aid your particular needs. *Check with him first.*

# SECTION THREE

# IRON PLAY

This section is devoted to the *long, medium,* and *short iron* full shots which are the ones which very often determine how well you are going to score.

As you will note in the following pages, these are the *accuracy* clubs, and in the execution of such shots you do not slug with these irons as you normally would with the wood clubs.

Many players, particularly the older ones, whose tee shots are somewhat shorter than that of their playing companions, have learned to become so accurate with their iron shots that they are consistently able to hit the ball close to the flag stick for an easy par or even a birdie, while their longer-hitting friends are spraying their slugged shots in all directions.

Accordingly, the more time you can give to the *study* and *practice* of the following pages on the science of *iron play,* the sooner you will find yourself listed in the low-handicap brackets.

Above all, don't *underclub* your shots. Don't try to make the club you use do more than it is capable of doing for the distance required.

## THIS GAME OF GOLF

### The Mental Attitude

In a previous section we stressed the need for professional instruction as the first step toward proficiency in the execution of your golf shots.

Of equal importance is your *mental attitude* throughout the entire period of each practice round or competitive play. To illustrate, the following are the four most important factors to keep in mind:

KNOWLEDGE   Seek competent professional teaching on a *regular* basis until you are convinced that you automatically know what to do in each situation as it arises. In addition, make sure that your teacher is convinced of your knowledge also.

CONCENTRATION   Careless play has no place in the proper execution of golf shots, and certainly is a detriment to good performance and good scoring. Most golfers play for pleasure, and the ones who get the most pleasure are the ones who score well.

Have all the fun you want—but the minute you pick up a club for *any* kind of shot, put everything out of your mind except to *concentrate* on the shot, and how you are going to execute it.

CONFIDENCE   While anyone, professional or amateur, occasionally makes a bad golf shot, put such things out of your mind immediately, except to vow that the same thing shall not happen again. If you have profited by your professional training, and concentrate properly on each shot, your confidence should be well established. *Never doubt your ability to perform well.*

RELAXATION With the first three factors mentioned above firmly established, there can be no *tension.* Your wrists and body muscles are completely relaxed, and your swing is smooth and rhythmic. As a result, your shots are everything you could hope for.

## IRON PLAY

In previous sections, the authors have fully recognized the value of the many fine instruction books covering various types of shots. In spite of this excellent information, however, these books very often may become a detriment to pupils wishing to improve their game, particularly those seeking initial instructions.

This is due in part to the fact that most golf instruction books attempt to cover as much of all golf shots as possible, from the driver to the putter. This would be fine provided the pupil would concentrate on *one* phase of the game at a time until mastering it.

But we continue to maintain that good golf instruction should start with *professional teaching,* followed by the study and memorizing of the step-by-step instructions. These sections segregate the various phases of the game, and we urge the student to give his full concentration to only *one step* at a time.

This section is devoted to *iron play,* which is considered by many to be the fine part of the game.

Iron clubs are designed more for accuracy than for long distance. A good golfer, therefore, does not "slug" with irons as he does with woods.

The Nos. 2 and 3 irons are called the long irons, and are the ones to use when the lie on the fairway does not permit the use of a wood club, although a maximum distance is required. Also, under windy conditions it is far safer to use a long iron than a wood club such as the No. 3 or No. 4.

The middle and short irons are the ones which help you to send your ball straight to the flag stick, within easy putting distance. Accuracy with these clubs helps many players, particularly older ones, to score well, though they may not be able to hit the greens in regulation strokes. In our opinion most golfers (including some of the better ones) fail to reach their objectives because they consistently "underclub." They *think* they hit a ball farther than they actually do. This generally causes them to slug their shot, often resulting in loss of timing, balance, and in defects in the direction of the ball's flight. Invariably the ball falls far short of the objective.

What is to be gained by this? Nothing but frustration. The golfer frequently remarks that he "didn't hit the ball." He is right, he didn't—properly.

Every golfer should learn his own distance capabilities for each iron club under all conditions of the elements. To start with, it is a good idea for him to use at least one number lower than he thinks for various distances, particularly where a full shot is required.

In making iron shots, only 80 to 85 percent of your power should be used if your stroke is to be smooth and rhythmic—and accurate. Bury your pride! Who knows what number club you have used unless you tell him? The important thing is to reach your objective.

A sample distance chart for basic iron play is contained in this book. Check this with your own performance, and make adjustments accordingly. Above all, see your PGA teaching professional for instruction on the science of iron play.

## THE LONG IRONS

These clubs are perhaps the most difficult ones, and to master them requires study and practice—and lots of it.

One must develop confidence in the ability to use them, and this can only come from a thorough knowledge of the fundamentals, and then practicing them until things begin to fall into place.

The illustrator, Dale Mead, is an exceptionally fine long iron player. A glance at the following photo should indicate why:

Because of Dale's height, and long arms, his hands are brought much higher at the top of his backswing than most players should attempt. However, if you can control the longer swing arc, O.K. But don't force a longer arc.

Keep your swing *smooth* and in *one piece*— and *don't hurry* the shot.

## What to Do

1. While approaching the ball in the fairway, determine all things necessary—the lie, impeding hazards, wind direction, club to use, etc. If a long iron is chosen:
   A. Take stance with the basic form as for wood clubs.
   B. Stand closer to the ball. (The shafts for irons are shorter than for wood clubs.)
   C. Grip the club firmly (since the shock of hitting the turf with the club face might cause it to turn in the player's hands, if the grip, particularly with the left hand, is too loose).
   D. A square stance is preferred for long iron shots, with feet spread not quite as wide as for wood shots. This allows a full backswing and pivot, with full turn of the shoulders to the right.
   E. Play the ball from a position in which it can be hit a downward blow—usually slightly to the right of the instep or heel of the left foot.
2. Start backswing (*low* and *slow*) with fully extended arms, until hands reach hip height, then cock wrists. *Don't hurry your swing.* "Easy does it."
3. With stance closer to the ball, the backswing is slightly more upright than for wood clubs. (This is a further aid to accuracy.)
4. At the top of the backswing, the hands are not brought much higher than the shoulders, although the position of the club is similar to that for the wood shots (pointing toward the target over the shoulder).
5. The downswing is started in the same manner as with the wood clubs, although the swing arc is much more vertical.
6. Keep the entire swing in one piece, and do not allow the head or body to sway.
7. The weight shifts to left on downswing, with majority of weight on inside of left foot just before impact with the ball. At the finish, 95 percent of weight should be on left foot. Do not "lock" the left leg.
8. At impact, the back of the left hand and palm of the right hand should be *square* to the line of flight. *Do not roll wrists to the left.*
9. Follow through low, with right arm fully extended, and finish with hands high.

## How to Do It

Address—with ball positioned slightly to right of left foot.
(Grip club firmly.)

Start backswing—*low* and *slow*—with fully extended arms. *Don't pick up the club sharply.* *Keep head still,* and swing in one piece.

Top of backswing. *Keep firm grip on club handle.*

Note extremely high position of hands for this illustrator's tremendous power (most beginners will not reach this far).

*Draw* arms and hands down with wrists still cocked. *Keep head still.*

Follow through with fully extended arms, and with *eye still on* the original ball position until *well after impact.*

Finish follow-through with hands high, and weight completely on left foot.

## Why You Do It

ITEM 1. This item should be self-explanatory, so concentrate on your course of action for your next shot before you arrive at your ball's position in the fairway.

ITEMS 1A and 1B. The stance is the same as for wood shots, except slightly closer to the ball, since the club shafts are somewhat shorter. Make sure that the hands are slightly *ahead* of the ball at address, and that *club shaft, hands,* and *arms* form a *straight line* from the left shoulder to the ball.

ITEM 1C. A loose grip with the left hand will invariably cause the club face to "open up" with the shock of impact with the ball and ground. A sliced shot is the natural result. Grip firmly with the left hand, and make sure that *both* hands are closely "welded" together.

ITEM 1D. Except for intentional hook or fade shots, a square stance is recommended. For older players, who have difficulty making a full shoulder turn to the right in the backswing, a slightly closed stance will help. Be sure the right foot is placed only a *few inches* back of the left in relation to the line of flight, however.

ITEM 1E. Playing the ball off the left heel, or slightly to the right of this point, assures hitting it at the *bottom* of the swing arc. While this gives the effect of hitting the ball a downward blow, actually in most instances you "sweep" the ball off the turf with the *long* irons, with little or no divot being taken.

ITEM 2. The most important phase of the swing with the long irons, as with most all clubs, is the first twelve to twenty-four inches of the start of the backswing. Keeping the club head low to the ground for this distance in the takeaway from the ball, and with fully extended arms, until the hands reach hip height, prevents picking up the club head sharply, and sets up a good body pivot.

ITEM 3. Since the shafts of iron clubs become progressively shorter as the loft of the club face increases, the swing arc becomes shorter and more upright.

ITEM 4. While it is true that the higher the hands are brought in the backswing, with the woods and long irons, the more power can be generated in the downswing, it is best for the average player to keep his swing *compact* and within his personal limits. Iron shots are made for accuracy more than for extra distance. You should not slug with irons. In fact, the swing for the long irons should be no harder than for *full* shots with the shorter irons.

ITEMS 5 and 6. Don't rush the backswing or downswing with the long irons. Keep it smooth, and in one piece. Above all, keep the head as still as possible, and don't lunge at the ball. Also, don't crouch too much in addressing the ball. "Stand tall," with only a slight flexing of the knees.

ITEM 7. With the hip turn to the left becoming the start of the downswing, the body weight automatically shifts to the left foot. Actually, the first move of the hips is slightly lateral (without body sway), followed by the turn of the hips as the weight shifts.

ITEM 8. At impact with the ball, the left arm *must* be in control, to guide the club head *through* the ball and out toward the target. The back of the left hand, palm of the right hand *must* face the target also. Rolling the wrists to the left causes a badly pulled shot.

ITEM 9. As for all full shots, follow through low with arms fully extended, particularly the right, until the hands raise naturally to a high finish. "Throw" the club head out toward the target after the hit. *Don't quit on the shot.*

## THE MIDDLE IRONS

### What to Do

1. As in all golf shots, as the ball is approached, mentally size up the situation and determine the things to do: distance to the flag stick on the green, club to use, etc.

2. Where a middle iron is indicated, select club of sufficient length for the distance required, based upon personal ability. (When in doubt, use at least one club length longer.)

3. Stance is slightly closer to the ball than for long irons, and is slightly more open.

4. Ball is positioned a few inches back of a line even with the left heel. In other words, more toward the center of the stance. The hands should be ahead of the ball.

5. Backswing is the same as for long irons (*low* and *slow*), with both arms fully extended until hands reach hip height. *Don't lift club abruptly.*

6. At this point wrists break, with left arm kept comfortably straight.

7. In pivoting to the right, keep knees fairly level instead of dipping the left knee (as for the longer club shots). The left heel is lifted only enough to make the action of the pivot comfortable, with slight pressure off the inside of the left foot.

8. At the top of the backswing, see that the head is *still* over the ball, and that a firm grip is kept on the club handle. *Don't stretch or strain on the backswing.*

9. Start the downswing the same as for the long irons, with left hip leading the turn to the left, and left foot coming down flat on the ground in a "sitting down" to the ball action. Do not "lock" the left leg, and keep the swing fluid throughout.

10. Wrists remain cocked until slightly below the hips, when they uncock with a snap, with both straight at impact with the ball.

11. Strike the ball a descending blow, taking divot after impact. Keep eye on ball until well after impact.

12. Follow through low with fully extended arms, and with the weight finishing on the left foot.

**How to Do It**

Address—with ball positioned a few inches to right of left heel.

Start backswing with fully extended arms until hands reach hip height.
*Don't lift club abruptly.*

Top of backswing.
Make sure that head is *still*, over the ball, and *keep left arm straight*.

"*Draw*" arm down, with wrists still cocked, until slightly below the hips. Left hip leads the turn as weight begins to shift to left foot.

Follow through with hands high, and weight finishing on left foot.

## Why You Do It

ITEM 1. When the lie of the ball is close enough to the green to require only a middle or short iron shot, it is doubly important to mentally determine the strategy for the shot to the target as you approach the ball. When you start to *execute* the shot, only one thing should be uppermost in your mind—hitting the ball as close to the flag stick as possible. Everything else should already have been decided.

ITEM 2. Don't try to reach your objective by underclubbing. Know *your own distances* for each club, through *practice*. Considering such factors as wind direction, condition and position of the green, etc., use the club that will *get you there*, even if it is one or more club lengths longer than you think you need. For most golfers (not professionals) their shots are more often *short* of the target than those which go past it. If you can hit your ball close to the flag stick, it *might* go in the cup, or at least end up close enough for a short putt. If you are consistently short with your shots, you lose both ways.

ITEMS 3 and 4. The club shafts for the middle irons are even shorter than for the long irons, so the stance is naturally closer to the ball. Also, since the swing arc is shorter and more compact, the stance becomes more open as the shorter irons are used. The ball being positioned a few inches to the right of the left heel permits the impact to occur *before* the bottom of the swing arc is reached. A divot is therefore taken after the ball is struck. With the hands slightly ahead of the club head, a properly lofted shot is assured, assuming the entire swing is well executed.

ITEMS 5 and 6. Keep the backswing smooth and unhurried, with the left arm and club shaft forming a straight line. Don't let the club head lag behind the hands during the takeaway, or catch on the grass during this process by grounding the club too firmly on the turf.

When the club head reaches approximately hip height, the wrists should break automatically, but this should be kept at a minimum. Keep the entire backswing smooth and in one piece, with the left arm kept comfortably straight throughout the swing.

ITEM 7. Since the middle and short irons are played more for accuracy than for distance, the body and shoulder turn becomes less, and the backswing more upright. Therefore, the knees remain fairly level, with very little lifting of the left heel during the pivot to the right.

Of the greatest importance is making sure that the *right* shoulder is *lower* than the left at address, and at the start of the backswing. The low right shoulder makes it easy to keep the right arm "hinged" and tucked in close to the right side for the start of a smooth backswing.

ITEM 8. Keep the head still and the eye on the ball. Fat hits are generally attributed to head movement and body sway. Part of this is frequently due to the player trying to slug the ball with too short a club for the distance required. In an effort to gain extra power in the hit, he stretches his backswing too far, causing head and body movement to the right. If in the process he also loosens the grip on the club handle, the club face alignment is changed, and only a miracle could allow him to regrip for a square club face at impact.

One should use only about 80 *percent* of his power with middle iron shots. It is far better to use a longer club than you think you need, and reach the target without forcing the shot.

Learn *your* distances for each club, and when in doubt use at least one club length more. Then watch the results. To prove this point, note that most players are more consistently *short* of their objective than over it.

ITEMS 9 and 10. The downswing for the middle irons starts with the left hip leading, followed by the turn of the shoulders. The arms are drawn downward, with the wrists still cocked until the hands are just below the hips. The club handle tip should then be pointing toward the ground, and the right elbow brought in close to the right front of the body. This is the start of the "uncoiling" of the right side muscles.

When the right side (hip, shoulder, and leg) is relaxed, and moves around to the target line, and the left side firms up, the weight shifts to the left foot, setting up a "wall of resistance" anchored in the left heel. As the wrists uncock with a snap, the club-head speed increases naturally, providing all the power necessary. Keep the swing "lazy" and fluid.

ITEMS 11 and 12. Since the swing for the middle irons is more vertical than for longer clubs, and impact with the ball is just *before* the bottom of the swing arc has been reached, a divot will be taken after impact with the ball. Hit the back of the ball *first;* the divot-taking follows. This points up the importance of keeping the head still and the eye on the ball until well after impact. Otherwise, a fat hit or sculled shot could result.

Following through low with fully extended arms will assure hitting *through* the ball instead of *at* it. It also assures shifting the weight fully to the left side. Finishing with the hands high indicates that all parts of the swing have been correct, with a good turn and tilt of the shoulders. It also assures getting the maximum distance from the hit, and helps promote accuracy of the ball's flight.

## THE SHORT IRONS

### Full Shots

### HIT THE TARGET

Because of the extreme importance the short iron clubs play in good scoring, when playing *full shots* with these clubs we believe the following points should be stressed before outlining the complete techniques in making these shots:

1. Don't underclub yourself. If in doubt, use one more club length.

2. Don't slug. The objective is *accuracy*, not extra distance.

3. Follow through *low*, and finish with the club head pointing to the target.

Again, Dale Mead shows the proper finish in his swing with the short irons. With the club head pointing to the target, where else can the ball go but *straight?*

## What to Do

1. Mentally review the necessary course of action as you approach your ball.
2. Line up your shot to the target, and determine the club to use.
3. Take an open stance, with weight even on both *heels and soles* of both feet. Don't lean forward on the soles alone.
4. Position of the ball should be more toward the center of the stance, which will be closer to the ball than for either the long or the middle iron shots. The hands should be *ahead* of the club head at address.
5. Use very little body turn. Both feet should be kept on the ground throughout the backswing. Sixty percent of the weight should be on the *left* foot.
6. Take the club back *low* and *slow*, with straight left arm. Use very little hip turn, but a full shoulder turn, until the chin touches the left shoulder.
7. Right elbow stays close to the body. Cock the wrists when hands reach hip height.
8. The short iron swing is very upright, but must be made from *inside* the line of flight.
9. Stretch left arm to full extent of your ability without straining, the same as for other iron shots.

10. On the downswing, left shoulder moves away from the chin, bringing the club down to the ball. At this point, the left leg begins to brace, and by bracing we do not mean to "lock" the left leg. Keep the swing fluid throughout.

11. Wrists begin to uncock at approximately hip height, snapping the club head down to the ball.

12. Stay *down to the ball*. Don't lift the left shoulder until well after impact.

13. Keep left side firm to hit against, with right arm slightly bent just before impact, and with palm of right hand *facing* the target. The right arm straightens after impact and on for the full follow-through.

14. Hit down sharply on the ball, taking divot after the hit.

15. Follow through low and fully, with club head pointing toward the target. Don't flip the club at the ball.

## How to Do It

Address—with ball positioned near center of stance.

Side view of open stance, with weight *even* on both feet.

*Don't lean forward on soles of feet alone.*

The downswing. *Stay down to the ball.* (Don't lift left shoulder.)

Side view of backswing at start.

Full backswing must be more *upright* than for longer iron shots, but must be made from *inside* the line of flight.

Follow through with club head pointing toward the target.

*Keep weight on left foot.*

## Why You Do It

ITEM 1. As the player comes closer to the green or target area, the accuracy of his shots becomes vitally important. Here is where the player who often does not hit the greens in the regulation number of strokes can overcome this problem and score well, *if* he can hit his ball to a point close to the flag stick for one putt. So it behooves him to plan his strategy carefully—i.e., the club to use, impeding hazards such as sand traps, trees, the slope of the green, etc. If you want to score well, this is the place to concentrate on the proper course of action.

ITEM 2. After lining up your shot to the target, make sure that your address position is also lined up correctly. If you are facing out of line with the intended flight direction, you can't expect the ball to go where you want.

ITEM 3. With the shorter irons, the backswing is shorter and more upright. An open stance is employed, therefore, with the left foot drawn back slightly from the intended line of flight. The weight should be *even* on both heels and soles of *both* feet because there will be very little hip turn, and to assure maintaining perfect balance.

To allow the weight to rest forward mostly on the soles would cause loss of balance, with the body thrown forward during the downswing. A hit from the outside in is the result, frequently causing a "shanked" shot (hitting the ball on the hosel of the club head), which is one of the most disgusting shots in the game. Ask any player!

ITEM 4. The ball must be struck with a downward firm stroke, and a divot taken, so it should be positioned toward the center of the stance. Since the shafts are shorter than for the middle and long irons, the stance is naturally closer to the ball. Correct address position finds the body inclined only a little, with the sole of the club head *flat* on the ground behind the ball. Don't lean forward so that the club head is resting on its heel, or stand so close or erect that it rests on the toe of the club head. The hands should also be *ahead* of the club head, with the left arm and club shaft forming a straight line to the left shoulder.

ITEM 5. Both feet remain on the ground throughout the backswing, with the weight resting mainly on the left foot. Since the backswing is more upright, there is very little body turn.

ITEMS 6 and 7. As for all full shots, the backswing is started by a push through the left arm, which is kept straight throughout the swing. For the shorter iron shots there is very little hip turn, but a *full* shoulder turn. The right elbow staying close to the body controls the plane of the backswing, and keeps the club head in proper alignment. Wrist-cocking takes place at approximately hip height, but is kept to a minimum of wrist break. Keep the swing in one piece.

ITEM 8. Taking the club head back low to the ground at the start of the backswing, with a straight left arm and proper shoulder turn, will assure taking it back inside the line of flight. Don't pick up the club sharply.

ITEM 9. Since most shots with a short iron are full shots involving a full backswing, the left arm should take the club head back as far as possible without straining. If the proper club has been selected for the distance required, the loft of the club head will prevent overshooting the target. Since the manufacturer built this loft in various clubs for the estimated distances to be expected from *full* shots, moreover, the force of the swing should be quite similar for all iron shots except the very short ones just off the green.

ITEM 10. At the start of the downswing, with the left shoulder moving away from the chin, the arms are again drawn down with the wrists still cocked. The full weight is then placed upon the left foot with the left leg beginning to brace, but not lock. *Keep the swing fluid.* Don't lunge at the ball.

ITEMS 11 and 12. The delayed uncocking of the wrists again provides the increased club-head speed to provide the proper power for the hit. *Stay down to the ball*—don't lift the left shoulder trying to "scoop" the ball up. After impact, the left shoulder will rise naturally.

ITEM 13. When the left side collapses instead of bracing, the left arm loses control and anything can happen, usually a badly pulled shot, or even a bad slice. The left arm should throw the club head out toward the target, with the palm of the right hand also facing this objective during impact. Keeping a firm left side throughout the downswing not only aids the flight direction but forces the right shoulder down, and brings the body in behind the shot for the required power.

ITEM 14. Hitting down sharply at the ball with a divot taken *after* the impact assures getting the backspin for the ball to rise for a good trajectory. For the shot to the green to hold when it lands close to the flag stick, this height is desirable. When the shot has not been made in this manner, and is instead scooped off the ground, there is too much danger of a topped or sculled shot that misses the objective entirely. ITEM 15. The low and full follow-through with the club head pointing toward the target after impact helps to assure a straight shot and the attainment of the required distance. Don't flip the club head at the ball! Hit *through* the ball, not *at* it.

## CLUB DISTANCES

The distance attained with various clubs will differ depending on several factors, including the player's age, physical condition, skill, and weather conditions.

The following chart shows the average distances expected under normal conditions. Check your own distances for each club, and record them in the space provided below. Then choose the club that will send your ball to the target without having to force the shot.

| CLUB USED | AVERAGE DISTANCE | YOUR DISTANCE |
|---|---|---|
| No. 1 Wood | 220 Yards | ——— |
| No. 2 Wood | 210 " | ——— |
| No. 3 Wood | 200 " | ——— |
| No. 4 Wood | 190 " | ——— |
| No. 5 Wood | 180 " | ——— |
| No. 2 Iron | 180 " | ——— |
| No. 3 Iron | 170 " | ——— |
| No. 4 Iron | 160 " | ——— |
| No. 5 Iron | 150 " | ——— |
| No. 6 Iron | 140 " | ——— |
| No. 7 Iron | 130 " | ——— |
| No. 8 Iron | 120 " | ——— |
| No. 9 Iron | 110 " | ——— |
| Wedge | 100 " | ——— |

Don't try to hit the ball at full strength. Bury your pride and use a longer club if necessary. After all, what difference does it make what club you use, as long as you hit the target?

The average distance for the *wedge* is shown as 100 yards. However, most professionals claim the maximum distance for the best accuracy is 75 yards.

## MORE ABOUT CLUB DISTANCES

You naturally hit a ball better and farther when you are fresh and relaxed.

When you are tired, and seem to be losing some of your distance, *don't press* and try to hit harder. *Swing easier.* A smooth, rhythmic swing may make up the difference.

Concentrate on *every shot*. Don't become lackadaisical or careless. Most poorly executed shots will cost you strokes which can never be recovered.

Remember what you have learned from your professional teacher, and use it. You paid for this teaching—so why not profit from it?

The average golfer cannot be expected to hit a ball with any club as far as a professional does. Learn *your* maximum distances for each club, and adjust your game accordingly.

Learn to play position. Maintain good ball control. Aim to keep your ball in the fairway.

Use one club length longer than you think you need. It is safe to assume that this will put your ball closer to the target more often than what may have been your past experience of being consistently short.

Swing smoothly on iron shots. Use only 80 to 85 percent of your power. Select the right club and *let IT do the work*.

# SECTION FOUR

# THE SHORT-SHORT GAME

This section covers the part of golf which most players agree is the most important. Certainly, the ability to master the *short-short* game will contribute the most toward good scoring.

Many players, particularly men, are capable of hitting good, long drives off the tee. They may also hit most of their shots very well from the fairway. But if they don't hit the greens in the regulation number of strokes, they will certainly be called upon to make short pitch shots, chips, or even the more difficult shots from a sand trap. Then comes that part of the game which accounts for one-half or more of all the strokes made in a total round of golf, *putting*.

Because she is generally a good student, and takes her practice sessions seriously, our lady golfer is frequently able to develop her short-short game to the point where she can overcome the loss of distance from her drives, or fairway woods and iron shots. Result: She is able to score well, in spite of this natural handicap.

This also applies to many older players, whose strength and suppleness of body have dwindled a little, so that they too must sacrifice some distance in their shots with the longer clubs.

Because of our intense desire to help all students of the game, we urge everyone to *study* this section carefully, and *practice* religiously until you too have mastered these all-important phases.

Above all, don't try to go it alone. See your PGA teaching professional regularly.

## THIS GAME OF GOLF

What does it mean to *you?*

Just how tough is this game of golf? Is it so complex that it is too difficult to learn, for the average beginner, or to improve, for those in the high handicap brackets? The simple answers are NO!

It is true that some progress faster than others, and some never quite reach the point where they become outstanding players. But anyone who is *willing* to take lessons from a good professional teacher, who will study and *memorize these teachings*, and who will *practice regularly*, can become a fairly good golfer in a relatively short time.

In what other sport can people of all ages continue to play—to get as much healthful exercise, or to meet so many interesting people? A sport where a man and his devoted wife can spend many happy hours together and receive untold benefits from every angle.

Consider the retired man or couple. They need never become bored with life, because golf provides most everything they could wish for to fill their days. Healthful exercise, good companionship, mental activity, a daily challenge, and a sense of accomplishment.

Another point is: Just how seriously must one take the game? The answer is, just as seriously as you wish to take it, except that one should never allow this or any other sport to make him tense, intolerant, unpleasant, or uncompanionable.

Golf is a game to enjoy, to have fun, and because it is so pleasantly engrossing, one can put everything else out of his mind, and be completely relaxed while playing it. It still requires concentration if you are to play it well, however.

Unlike the person who says, "I don't want to take this game so seriously," play it to the hilt, with all of the ability you have. It is certain that you will enjoy it more, and have more fun, because of the rewarding results of your efforts.

## THE SHORT-SHORT GAME

Without doubt we have all heard the expression, "drive for show, and putt for dough." And how true it is!

We all know how many times we have made a good long drive off the tee, another straight second shot (just short of the green), and then for some reason the pitch to the green is either too short or too long, and we end up taking three putts to get the ball in the cup. Has this not happened to you?

Four shots have been made from the pitch shot to putting the ball in the cup, which is *twice* as many as it took to get from the tee to the near edge of the green. For a par four hole this means a double bogey. Have too many of these and your score is ruined.

Contrary to this, if you can learn to pitch and chip the ball reasonably close to the flag stick, you stand a good chance of dropping the ball for a par score. On the shorter par four holes, and most of the par five holes, a well-placed pitch shot, close to the flag stick, affords the player an opportunity to birdie the hole.

One of the most certain ways to improve pitching ability is to practice the shot from various distances to the target. From such practice it is soon possible to learn the range for each club used, and get an idea as to the length of the backswing necessary for the needed distance.

Of course, the first step is to have your teaching professional instruct you in proper form and technique. Next, practice the stroke in your own backyard until you can place the ball within easy putting distance of your target most of the time.

The author has spent many pleasant hours in his own backyard, pitching to two six-foot circles set sixty feet apart. In the center of each circle, a one-pound coffee can is sunk just below the grass surface, with a hole centered in the bottom of the can. An old mop stick is inserted to serve as a flag stick.

Pitching for about an hour at a time, it should not take long before one can place most of his practice shots to within the six-foot circle. Even though the grass surface near this circle is not the same as a putting green, adjustments can be made in your stroke to compensate.

Try this, and see how much it can improve your pitch-and-run shots. Chip shots can also be practiced in the same manner. Remember, when you can place your ball within a six-foot circle such as described, you will have only *a three-foot putt or less to the cup.*

The full hit backspin, or the cut shots, are more difficult, and perhaps should be tried at the practice range of the golf course, to save possible damage to your own lawn. These are valuable shots in hitting over trees, out of heavy rough or sand, or to pitch over a trap where there is little room for the ball to run on the green to the cup.

Playing out of sand traps is a harrowing experience for most high handicap players, and is the place where more shots are wasted than any other place on the golf course, except perhaps the putting green. Even though these trap shots are more difficult for the average player than some others, they can be learned when one develops the proper coordination of mind, muscles, and nerves, which control perfect timing.

Finally, all the excellence of good pitch shots, chips, and sand trap play will be of little consequence if one cannot putt the ball into the cup with reasonable regularity. With proper initial professional instruction, and a little regular practice, *anyone* can learn to putt well.

This section attempts to cover the basic principles of the various golf shots involved in what we choose to call the Short-Short Game. Proficiency in their execution is necessary for good scoring.

## THE PITCH SHOT

### With Pitching Wedge

#### What to Do

To begin with, there are many types of golf shots which can be made with the pitching wedge. We shall confine this outline of the techniques, however, to the type of short pitch shots most generally used.

1. The basic fairway pitch shot.
(For distances of approximately thirty to fifty yards.)
2. The punch pitch shot.
(For hitting into headwinds or crosswinds.)
3. The cut shot pitch.
(For hitting over bunkers or other low hazards.)

*For the basic fairway pitch shot:*

A. Position the ball a few inches to the right of the left heel.
B. Stand closer to the ball than for normal full iron shots, and use a slightly open stance.
C. Shorten the grip on the club handle.
D. At address, keep the majority of the weight on the left side.
E. The hands should be *ahead* of the ball at address. Grip the club handle lightly, but grip *firmly* with the last three fingers of the left hand.
F. Keep the backswing "short and crisp" with straight left arm.
G. Use very little body turn, but almost full shoulder turn. The entire swing is strictly a *hand, arm,* and *wrist* action.
H. Left knee dips forward, as right knee braces (but not locks), and with *both heels remaining on the ground.*
I. Wrists cock at approximately hip level.
J. At start of downswing, shift weight to left side.
K. Now pull down with left arm (which is kept straight), and with wrists still cocked.

L. Keep *head and body still*, with the master eye *glued* on the ball.
M. When the hands drop a little below hip level, start uncocking the wrists. Left hip moves out of the way as arms bring hands into hitting position.
N. *Stay down to the shot,* with hands leading the club head *down* and *through* the ball.
O. At impact, the *back* of left hand and *palm* of right hand face the target.
P. Keep the *head down,* and *eye on the ball,* until well *after* impact.
Q. After impact, the right arm straightens for the full follow-through.
R. Throw the club head out straight toward the target.
S. Finish follow-through with hands fairly high, and the body facing the target. *Don't quit on the shot,* or stub the club head into the ground behind the ball.

*For the punch pitch shot:*

A. Position the ball a little more toward the right foot.
B. Use the same open stance.
C. Keep the weight on the *left side* throughout the shot.
D. Keep the hands *well ahead* of the ball.
E. Use the same execution for the backswing and downswing, except the backswing is slightly more upright.
F. Stroke *through* the ball *crisply,* with the hands *low,* and with the left arm *straight* and *firm.*
G. Keep the follow-through low, and the club head *pointing toward the target* at the finish.

*For the cut shot pitch:*

A. Use the same ball position as for the punch pitch shot.
B. Use *more* of an open stance, with the weight *kept* on the left side.
C. Lay the club face back open, with the hands *slightly behind* the ball.
D. Take a short upright backstroke, with the wrists breaking sharply.
E. Use *no body action,* except that left knee

"rolls" to the right on backswing, and right knee to the left on downswing.

F. On the downswing, cut across the ball from the *outside* of the intended line of flight. Aim slightly to the *left* of the target.

G. Bring the open club face into and *under* the ball at impact.

H. Swing *through* the ball, with the wrists again breaking sharply in a "flipping" action, with the hands finishing higher than for the "punch" pitch.

I. Use this shot *only* if the ball is *sitting up well* in the grass. Don't try this shot off *hard ground* or when the ball is sitting in a divot or a tight lie.

The player is often called upon to hit over a tree which is directly in line with his objective. The same basic technique is employed for getting over this hazard as is described above for the cut shot pitch, except that this shot requires a strong full swing instead of the flipping action for the shorter cut shot.

There are several other trouble shots where the pitching wedge, or even the sand wedge, can be used to get you out of trouble and back on the beam, such as shots from heavy rough, from normal rough bordering the fairway, and from wet, soggy ground.

These shots are more adequately described in the section "Professional Tips," which also includes techniques for overcoming problems caused by abnormal lies—corrections for various errors in execution, etc.

It is perhaps right and proper to credit the *pitching wedge* with being one of the most versatile clubs the player can use to help him improve his score.

Once you have learned to use this club properly, you will gain the confidence needed to carry off your shots with it, and will call upon it more and more.

The quickest way to bring this about is to see your PGA teaching professional *now,* and then *practice—practice—practice!*

## How to Do It

Address, and open stance.
Hands *slightly ahead* of the ball.

Arm and body position just before impact with ball.
*Stroke crisply.*

Backswing, more upright, with very little body turn. Stroke mostly with arms and hands. Keep weight on left side.

Follow through with straight left arm, and with both arms *fully extended.*

For lofting ball over high trap lip, where there is very little green surface to land on, use open stance and club face, and play a cut shot. *Stroke firmly, into and under the ball.*

## Why You Do It

ITEM 1A. This is the ball position for most of the shots which are made with every iron club from the No. 2 iron to the wedge, from *level fairway* lies under normal conditions. Most fairway wood shots from similar lies are played from this ball position.

To keep changing the ball position for various clubs of the above range would require you to change the arc of your swing and the manner in which you hit the ball.

Obviously, the ball position must be changed for playing uphill or downhill lies, or when playing shots against a headwind, out of heavy rough, for cut shots, etc.

ITEM 1B. When playing the short pitch shot the stance is quite narrow, since there will be little if any body motion. The feet are spread only a few inches apart at address.

Since the distance for such short pitch shots will not require a full swing, the stance will be more open than for longer iron shots, which automatically shortens the length of the backswing.

When playing this short pitch shot with a pitching wedge, which has a shorter club shaft than most of the iron clubs, the stance will be much closer to the ball. Assuming the stroke into the ball is correct (in theory, the closer the stance is to the ball, the more loft that can be expected in its flight).

When taking the stance, position the *left foot* first, in an open position to an imaginary line parallel to the line of flight. Then place the right foot *about four inches* forward of the left. The left foot is thus kept in a more constant position, and the ball is automatically positioned correctly for most shots.

For the longer pitch shots, since more body turn will be used for a full swing, the stance will be only slightly open. The swing for such *full* pitch shots is the same as one uses for a No. 8 or No. 9 iron. The loft of the club face takes care of the distances to be expected for each of these clubs, provided the swing tempo and execution are uniformly the same.

ITEM 1C. For the shorter pitch shots, since the backswing will be less, the hands should be moved down on the grip. This helps promote good club control, and keeps the backswing compact and in one piece.

ITEM 1D. At address, the majority of the weight should be on the *left side*. By keeping body movement to a minimum, and the weight to the left, there is less chance of body sway and a resulting fat hit or sculled shot.

ITEM 1E. Of the greatest importance is the matter of keeping the hands *ahead* of the ball at address. With the hands and weight forward, the player can more easily hit *down* and *through* the ball. In addition, these short pitch shots are not played for *distance* but for *accuracy*. Therefore the club handle is gripped lightly, with the exception that it should be *firmly* gripped with the *last three fingers* of the left hand. This will prevent the club face from opening up with the shock of hitting the turf after impact with the ball.

ITEM 1F. Accuracy is aided further by keeping the backstroke short, crisp, and compact. This is quite different from the slower and more complete backswing when the body is being coiled for a *power* hit. One must also remember that the left arm is the "guiding" arm for the swing in *all* golf shots. When it is allowed to collapse, anything can happen—except a good solid hit.

ITEM 1G. In the backstroke, as the club is taken back for a more upright short swing, the shoulders tilt and make *almost* a full turn, but there is little or no turn of the hips. Therefore, the entire swing is mainly performed with the hands, arms, and wrist action.

ITEM 1H. Instead of standing stiff when making the backstroke, the left knee dips forward as the right knee braces, but with *no body sway*. Since there will be a minimum of body movement, *both heels should remain on the ground,* which further prevents body sway.

ITEM 1I. The cocking of the wrists takes place at about hip level, but since the backswing is shorter this is kept at a minimum, where only a one-half or three-quarter backswing is used.

ITEM 1J. Shifting the weight back to the left side at the start of the downswing assures hitting down and through the ball at impact, instead of scooping the shot.

ITEM 1K. The straight left arm is then pulled down, with the tip of the club handle pointing toward the ground, and with the wrists still cocked slightly. The right elbow has been brought in close to the right hip. All this helps to control the plane of the downswing, and assures a crisp, solid hit.

ITEM 1L. To allow the head to move on either the backswing or the downswing encourages body sway, resulting in topped or scuffed shots. The head should be considered the axis around which the swing arc is built, even for the short pitch shots. Also, to take the eye off the ball is *fatal*. You can't hit what you can't see! (unless you have an exceptional memory).

ITEM 1M. Delaying the uncocking of the wrists until the hands drop below hip level assures a well-controlled, crisp hit at impact.

As the arms bring the hands into a hitting position, the left hip moves out of the way to ensure a smooth downstroke and follow-through.

ITEM 1N. Staying down to the shot, with the hands *leading* the club head down and through the ball, assures a solid, crisp impact. When one raises the body at this point only a scooped or topped shot can result.

ITEM 1O. The back of the left hand and the palm of the right hand *must* face the target at impact, and be kept there until the start of the follow-through. To allow the right hand to overtake the left at this point results in a rolling of the wrists to the left, closing the club face, and causing a pulled shot to the left. The left hand and arm *must stay in control.*

ITEM 1P. Raising the head, and taking the eye off the ball, just at the point of impact, can only result in a ruined shot, mostly by topping or scuffing. *Keep the head down.* Don't be too anxious to see where the ball is going. If you will only concentrate on what you are doing, and do it well, the ball will usually go where you want it to. Peeking is *fatal!*

ITEMS 1Q and 1R. The straightening of the right arm, while maintaining control of the left, in the follow-through, throws the club head out straight at the target. When this is done, where else can the ball go but straight to your objective?

ITEM 1S. As the body swings around to face the target, the hands raise fairly high in the follow-through. This assures a smooth, full finish, and good balance of the body. Above all, don't quit on the shot, *stubbing the club head into the ground* behind the ball. This is the quickest way to scull a shot, and lose complete control of the ball's flight in distance and direction.

*For the punch pitch shot:* This type of pitch shot must be played differently than a normal pitch, particularly under windy conditions, when you want to hit the ball low. The punch pitch is then the shot to use.

ITEM 2A. The ball is positioned a little more toward the right foot, because you want to keep the flight *low.*

ITEM 2B. The stance is open because the backswing is to be *short* and *crisp.*

ITEMS 2C and 2D. It is essential to keep the weight on the left side throughout the entire backswing and downswing, and the hands well ahead of the ball. To overlook these points could cause a badly sculled shot.

ITEM 2E. The backswing is short and crisp, but more upright than for a normal pitch shot, because you are going to punch down on the ball with the hands lower than usual at the point of impact.

ITEM 2F. The downstroke is *crisp,* with the club head descending when it meets the ball. The hands are low, and the left arm is kept straight and firm, with firm wrists. This assures hitting into and through the ball sharply.

ITEM 2G. Keep the follow-through *short* and *low,* since the trajectory of the shot will be low, particularly to reduce the effect of headwind or crosswind, when playing this shot under these conditions. With the club head pointing

to the target at the finish, the ball's flight should also be straight to your objective.

*For the cut shot pitch:* The cut shot pitch provides a high, "soft" trajectory, with the ball "floating" up to the objective. It is a delicate shot, requiring the *utmost concentration.*

ITEMS 3A, 3B, and 3C. The same ball position is used as for the punch pitch shot, with the stance more open, because the backstroke is shorter, and much more upright, than for a normal pitch shot. The club face is "layed back" open, with the hands *slightly behind* the ball. This causes the club head to cut *into* and *under* the ball from *outside* the line of flight. The weight must be *kept* on the left side.

ITEM 3D. Early in the short upright backswing, the wrists break sharply, to create an upright swing plane, which allows the club head to travel into and under the ball as described above.

ITEM 3E. *No body action* is used. "Rolling" the left knee to the right on backswing, and the right knee to the left on downswing, prevents body sway.

ITEMS 3F and 3G. On downswing, by cutting into and under the ball from outside the intended flight line, a clockwise spin is imparted to the ball. Therefore one should aim slightly to the left of the target.

ITEM 3H. Swinging *through* the ball, with the wrists breaking sharply in a "flipping" action, and with the hands finishing high, provides the loft and "floating" action to the ball's trajectory.

ITEM 3I. Since you must be sure to get the club head *under* the ball at impact, it must be *sitting up well* in the grass for the cut shot to be successful. If this shot should be tried off hard ground, or when the ball is in a tight lie or divot, the sole of the club head may bounce into the ball, causing a skulled or topped shot.

The cut shot is not one to be *afraid* of, but one to be *mastered.* Once this has been accomplished, it will get you out of trouble many, many times.

## THE CHIP SHOT
### What to Do

1. Select club, either No. 5, 6, or 7 iron, depending upon preference, and the roll on the green to be desired. By "hooding" the club face, a pitching wedge is also effective for chip shots to the flag stick.
2. Take an open stance, close to the ball, and choke down on the club grip.
3. Position the ball in the center of the stance, with club head square to the target, or slightly closed. Keep hands well *ahead* of club head at address.
4. KEEP weight on the left foot. Also keep head still, and the eye on the ball.
5. Take club head back *low* to the ground, with arms and hands only, using *no* body action. Use a minimum of wrist break. Keep right elbow *close* to the body.
6. Don't scoop the shot. The left arm and hand leads the club head down and *through* the ball on the downstroke.
7. Make sure the left hand moves past the ball, without the left wrist breaking. Wrists must not "roll" at impact.
8. For a "running" shot, pick a spot on the green for the ball to land (usually about one-fourth the distance) on a *level* green, with a roll to the cup for the balance. Adjust this landing spot as necessary, for uphill or downhill rolls where the green has such slopes.
9. Strike the ball with a lot of *right* hand, using a putting stroke.
10. For a quick-stopping chip, open the club face and use a more upright backstroke, taking the club head to the outside of the direction line. This creates an outside-in downstroke, across the ball for greater backspin.
11. Have the feeling of hitting against a straight left arm, with follow-through low and smooth.
12. Finish with the club face, the back of the left hand, and the palm of the right hand square to the target.

If you have just missed the green in the regulation number of strokes (two or three strokes for the par four and par five holes respectively) this is the little stroke-saver which may put your ball to within easy distance for *one* putt.

### How to Do It

Address and ball position.

Backstroke. Take club head back *low* to ground, with *arms and hands only*, using a putting stroke, and with a minimum of wrist break.

At impact, strike ball with lots of right-hand action, using a putting stroke for a running shot.

For a quick-stopping shot, open club face, and use "upright" backstroke.

Take club head back *outside* the direction line. This swing will cut the club across the ball, causing a backspin that brings the ball to a quick stop.

## Why You Do It

ITEM 1. The chip shot is a lofted putt, and is the type of shot which is generally the most effective when the ball lies just a *short distance* off the green. The loft is *low*, but must be sufficient to land the ball *on the green* for a run up to the flag stick.

When the shot is not sufficient to reach the green, and at a point far enough on this surface for an accurate roll to the objective, it lands on the fringe, or (frog hair) just bordering the green where the grass is a little longer, and where occasional divots are present. This generally results in a quick stop of the ball, or even a deflection of its direction. Result: either a second chip is required, or at least a long putt (maybe *three* of them).

When there is any doubt that the ball will land safely on the green for a good run to the cup, or where there is little room between the lie of the ball and the flag stick, use a *pitching wedge* for a short, more lofted chip. (The wedge is also effective for better ball control on *downhill* chips.) Otherwise, the club to use will be a No. 5, 6, or 7 iron, depending upon preference.

ITEM 2. The stance will be open, since the backstroke will be short. It will also be quite *close* to the ball, similar to a putting stance, which aids in keeping the club head in the proper direction line throughout the entire stroke. Choking down on the grip makes it easier to hit the ball properly, which further increases control.

ITEM 3. The ball is positioned near the center of the stance, because you are going to punch or bump the ball rather than try to scoop it. Generally, the club face should be square to the target, although a slightly closed club face may reduce the chance for backspin to occur sufficiently to restrict the ball's run on the green.

Of the greatest importance is the matter of keeping the hands well *ahead* of the club head at address, and throughout the entire stroke, which will assure that the ball will be struck *first* sharply, then the turf. When the club head passes the hands, scooping the shot generally is the result.

ITEM 4. Keep the weight on the left side throughout the *entire* stroke. Shifting the weight

increases the club-head speed, and affects the precision of the stroke. The head must be kept *still*, and the eye *fixed* on the ball at all times. This is a delicate precision shot, where absolute control of contact with the ball is necessary for proper direction and distance. Since this is of vital importance, to look up is *fatal*.

ITEM 5. The chip is an exaggerated putt, so the club head is taken back *low to the ground* with *no body action*. This shot is performed with the arms and hands only, and with a minimum of wrist break. (Some professionals prefer the "all-wrist" method, with the hands kept over the ball at all times, as a means of controlling the club face position.) We recommend using a minimum of wrist break, however, because for most golfers, to lift the club abruptly on the backswing, and snap the wrists on the downstroke, often results in scooping the ball up, instead of making a *crisp* stroke *through* the ball, which is much more to be desired. Keeping the right elbow *close to the right hip* provides tight control of the stroke.

ITEM 6. Don't scoop the shot, or try to *lift* the ball up. With the straight left arm and hand *leading* the club head *down* and *through* the ball *crisply*, the loft of the club face will lift the ball sufficiently for your purpose.

ITEM 7. If the left hand moves past the ball without the left wrist breaking, the normal loft of the club face will provide the proper flight and desired amount of roll for a running chip. When the wrists "roll" at impact, the ball will have a tendency to run sharply after landing on the green. Keep the right hand *under* the left, to keep the club face *square to the direction line*.

ITEM 8. Only through continual practice can one become reasonably accurate in landing his ball at the proper distance for a safe run to the cup. This landing point must obviously be adjusted for uphill or downhill chip shots, or where the green is either extra hard, or soft from excessive watering or rainy weather. It is therefore wise to walk up on the green to the flag stick to check the condition of the surface before making the chip shot. This inspection will help to determine what club to use for either a quick-stopping or running chip.

ITEM 9. Since the chip shot is actually an exaggerated putt, the stroke is similar to a putt, except that it is *more crisp,* with a lot of right-hand action against a *firm* left arm. The club head goes sharply *through* the ball, finishing in the follow-through, *pointing straight at the target.*

ITEM 10. For the quick-stopping chip, opening the club face and taking the club head back with an upright backswing, outside the line of flight, is similar to the cut shot pitch, except that the backswing is shorter because less distance is involved. Aim slightly to the *left* of the target for the same reason. The backspin of the ball coming off the open club face will impart a left-to-right spin after the landing.

ITEM 11. Unlike the regular cut shot, there is no flipping action of the wrists in the follow-through. The stroke is *crisp* and *low,* with straight left arm. The farther the right hand is placed *under* the left at impact, the softer the ball will land on the green. The right hand must *never* roll past the left at impact, or in the follow-through, for a *quick-stopping* chip. On the contrary, this would cause the ball to run.

ITEM 12. Once again, for direction accuracy, make sure that during the impact, and in the follow-through, the *club face,* the *back* of the *left hand,* and the *palm* of the *right hand* are *facing* the target.

## THE SAND TRAP SHOT

### What to Do

1. For normal trap shots, determine:

   A. The distance to the flag stick.

   B. How high is the lip of the trap in front of the ball?

   C. Is the sand wet or dry?

   D. Is the ball sitting up well, or buried?

2. If sand is dry, and ball sitting up well, anchor the feet *firmly* and stand well over the ball. Keep the weight on the left side.

3. Grip the club handle low, and play the ball off the *left heel,* with an open stance. *Do not ground your club head.* It is against the rules of the U.S.G.A.

4. Open the club face and take an exceedingly upright backswing, usually a three-quarter swing. Aim slightly to the *left* of the target. Take club head back *outside* the flight line.

5. Keep left arm straight, and cock wrists sharply.

6. Keep right elbow close to the body on the backswing.

7. On the downswing, cut across the ball from the outside in.

8. Hit the *sand* approximately one to two inches *behind* the ball, depending upon the texture of the sand, and the distance required for the shot. Keep the eye *fixed* on *this spot in the sand,* not the *ball.*

9. *Don't stub the club head into the sand.* Follow through *completely.* Adjust the swing and the force of the stroke, with the distances required.

10. For a buried lie, close or hood the club face at address by moving the hands ahead of the club head and playing the ball back toward the right foot a little. Swing harder than normal. *Open* the club face where *quick stop* is desired. Break wrists sharply in backswing, and stroke firmly with *lots of right hand,* entering sand as close as possible behind ball, with slicing action.

11. On all sand trap shots, *stay down to the ball.*

12. Where the front lip of the trap is low, and the ball is *sitting up well,* on *wet sand,* a chip shot may be employed, or even a putter used, but *hit the ball cleanly and firmly, not the sand behind it.* Play the ball to the right of the center of the stance for these shots.

13. On all trap shots, *make sure you get out in one stroke.* If the trap lip is too high, and the ball too close to the lip, *play safe,* and aim for a lower point of the lip, to assure getting out and on the green.

## How to Do It

Address—Front view, with ball sitting up well on dry sand. Open stance and club face. Play ball opposite *left heel*.

Address—Side view. Anchor feet firmly in sand. Be sure to smooth out foot and stroke marks after making shot.

Address—For buried lie. Play ball off right foot. Close club face, and be sure hands are *ahead* of the ball.

Take sharp upright backswing.

On the downswing, cut across the ball from the *outside* of direction line.

Aim to *left* of target, hit sand about one to two inches behind the ball, and *follow through completely*.

*Don't stub club head into the sand.*

## Why You Do It

ITEMS 1A, 1B, 1C, and 1D. When your ball lands in a greenside sand trap, the first thing you should do before attempting to make your shot is to size up the situation carefully. Don't just grab a club out of your bag, rush over to your ball, and whale away at it.

Take time to determine the best way to get out, and as close as possible to the flag stick. It can be done, you know! There is really *no reason to fear* a sand trap shot. All it takes is a little know-how, and confidence. Even the pros get into these hazards occasionally, but they *know* how to get out of them, and *so can you.*

First, check the points outlined on page 89. Then select the club to properly execute the shot in the manner described, and make your shot. If you will study the techniques outlined, and *practice* religiously, it won't be long before you will become a fine trap player. It is easier than you think!

ITEM 2. If the sand is *dry,* and the ball sitting up well, anchor the feet *firmly* by twisting them around in the sand until they are below the loose sand on top and feel as though they are on solid footing. This is to prevent the feet from slipping, with possible loss of balance and body sway, while executing the shot.

Stand well over the ball, with the weight *kept on the left side* throughout the swing. This is due to the fact that the backswing will be short and very upright and, with the weight to the left, the club head will cut across and *through the sand,* in *back* of the ball, in a firm but smooth stroke, instead of trying to "scoop" the ball up.

ITEM 3. The club handle should be gripped low on the leather, because the backswing will be short and upright. In addition, by digging the feet into the sand, they will be a few inches *lower* than for a normal fairway shot on level ground. The ball will therefore be that much higher than the feet, and closer to the hands, and this requires a sharp and short swing plane.

At address, the club head should be held behind the ball, and slightly above the sand to prevent grounding it, which is against the rules.

The stance is open, which makes it easier to control the shot, taking the club head back *outside* the flight line on the backswing, and cutting across to the *inside* on the downswing. Applying this cut into the *sand behind the ball* prevents slicing into the sand too deeply, or stubbing the club head into the sand and stopping it there. The open stance also allows the left hip to move out of the way on the downswing, assuring a *full follow-through.*

Playing the ball forward off the left heel, or even off the left instep or toe, compensates for the inch or more behind the ball the club head will enter the sand, as opposed to a normal fairway iron shot, where the ball is positioned slightly to the right of the left heel. This enables the impact to be made at, or slightly before, the bottom of the swing arc.

ITEM 4. The open club face enables the player to slice through the sand in back of the ball, and *under* it, instead of digging the club head into the sand. It also provides the desired loft to the shot for clearing the lip of the trap, and for settling quickly on the green.

The explosion shot should be a smooth, easy stroke, never made with full force. Therefore, the backswing is short, and sharply upright. The open stance assures taking the club head back *outside* the flight line. Because the downstroke will also be from the outside in, and the stance and club face are open, a left-to-right spin will be imparted to the ball. Therefore, one should aim slightly to the *left* of the target.

ITEM 5. With the open stance, the position of the right hip at address helps to control the hands from coming back in too flat a swing arc, and aids in a quick cocking of the wrists. The left arm, however, must be kept straight.

ITEM 6. Keeping the right elbow close to the body assures breaking the wrists early in the backswing, making it sharply upright.

ITEM 7. Since one must slice the sand *in back of* and *under* the ball on the downswing, this stroke must be made from *outside* the flight line. The *left hand and arm* lead the club head down and *through* the sand, smoothly but *firmly.*

ITEM 8. It is the *sand* that lifts the ball as the club head cuts under the ball one to two inches in back, depending upon the flight distance required. The club head makes *no contact with the ball itself.* To do so would result in picking it off too cleanly, probably sending it completely over the green to the other side. So the eye must be fixed on the proper spot to hit into the *sand*.

ITEM 9. Only a miracle will get the ball out of the trap when the club head is stubbed into sand and stopped there. *Follow through completely*, finishing with the club head fairly high. Only through *practice* will one be able to judge the amount of backswing, and the force of the swing necessary for various distances required. Such practice is *well worth the effort*.

ITEM 10. For a partly buried lie, the club face is closed or "hooded" at address, with the hands *ahead* of the club head. This reduces the chance of the rounded sole of the sand wedge to skim across the top of the sand and skull the shot. Instead the club head will cut deeper into the sand under the ball, and this requires a little more force in the swing. Also, playing the ball back toward the right foot a little assures hitting *through* the sand with a *downward* blow. In contrast, in a buried lie, where the flag stick is close to the near edge of the green, and a quick stop is desired, the club face must be *open*. Breaking the wrists early makes the backswing sharply upright. This creates a sharply vertical downswing, wth the *right hand* driving the club head down into the sand behind the ball in a slicing action. Hitting the sand as close as possible to the ball will "pop" the ball out with more backspin than with the normal trap shot.

ITEM 11. On all trap shots, it is essential to *stay down to the ball* instead of lifting the head, or trying to scoop the ball up by raising the body. *Flex the knees, and keep the head still.*

ITEM 12. On wet, compacted sand, with the ball sitting up well, and the front lip of the trap *low*, one may use a sand wedge, or instead may prefer to chip out. Either shot can be carried off successfully if executed properly. If a wedge is chosen, the club face is opened wide, and the club taken back *low* to the *outside* of the direction line. On the downswing, the club head enters the sand about an inch behind the ball, cutting under it *slightly* but not digging into the sand. The downstroke is naturally made from the outside in. Above all, make sure that the club head cuts *through* the sand behind the ball, and does not strike the ball first or a skulled shot will result.

If a chip shot is preferred *use an 8 iron, not a sand wedge*. Be sure to hit the ball *first*

cleanly in the same manner as when playing a chip shot off the grass. *Never* try a chip shot out of *dry, light sand*.

If the trap is fairly flat, and the front lip also low and flat, a putter may be used with good success. The ball is positioned similar to a regular putt on the green. Strike the ball cleanly, however, and with the *toe* of the club head. This will tend to reduce backspin of the ball and provide a better roll.

ITEM 13. Landing in a trap does not necessarily mean that you will lose an extra stroke on that particular hole—*if you make sure that you get out in one stroke*, and as close to the flag stick as possible.

There is no percentage in taking chances, however, particularly where the ball is too close to a high bank of the trap. Instead, *play safe*, and aim away from the target, toward a point where the trap lip is lower, if this should be possible, enabling you to get out, and on the green.

Even if you do have a longer putt, you *might* sink it. If you don't get out of the trap the first time, you have lost a stroke anyway, *maybe two*.

### THINGS TO REMEMBER ABOUT TRAP SHOTS:

The trap shot isn't as hard as you might think!

Twist the feet in the sand to assure a firm footing.

Stand over the ball, and *stay down to the shot*.

Fix the eye on the spot in the *sand* behind the ball, *not the ball*.

For most trap shots, take a sharp upright backswing *outside the target line*.

Stroke *under* and *through* the sand *under* the ball.

*Follow through completely. Don't stub the club head into the sand.*

Hit *shallow* and *farther behind* the ball to float it out with very little backspin.

Hit *shallow* and *quite close*, to stop the ball quickly *with* backspin.

Hit deeper, and farther behind the ball, for more run to the ball.

*Play safe*, and get out in *one stroke*.

## TIPS ON PUTTING

### What to Do

1. First, examine the grass, and the slope of the green, in the direct line of your putt as follows:
   A. For foreign matter such as leaves, twigs, etc.
   B. For repairable depressions or divots. Use wooden tee for repairs.
   C. Which way is the grass grain growing? Toward your line of putt—away from it, or across the line, either left to right, or right to left.
   D. Is the putt uphill or downhill? How much?
   E. Is there a lateral slope to right, or left?
   F. Is the grass on the green closely mowed, or a little high?
   G. Is the green hard or soft? Wet or dry?
   H. If "casual water" is in line with your putt, or where your ball rests, it is permissible to move it without penalty, to a point no nearer the cup, which has no water in your line. U.S.G.A. *rules*.
2. Sight the line of putt from in back of the ball.
3. Pick out a spot on the green about five or six inches from the cup, to which you will aim your putt.
4. Take stance *with weight on the left side, and with toes of both feet even* on the line parallel to where you want the ball to travel.
5. Stand close enough to the ball so that the putter blade is *flat* on the ground, and with your "master" eye right over the ball. Keep hands *close* to your body.
6. Grip club at top of handle. (Don't choke down on the club.)
7. Grip club handle with both hands close together, using reverse overlap (left forefinger extended down, and outside the last two or three fingers of the right hand). The back of left hand, and palm of right hand should face the target, with both hands slightly *under* the club handle.
8. *Remove all thoughts* from your mind except making the proper putting stroke. *Relax*.
9. Position the ball about one or two inches to the right of the left toe.
10. Keep the *head still, and the body motionless*.
11. Keep putter blade *low to the ground* on backswing. Gauge the backswing distance by the length of the putt. A good rule of thumb is to place both feet together, then move the right foot to the right, the width of that foot, and bring the putter blade back to the outside of the right foot for a *ten-foot putt*. Move the right foot one more width for a twenty-foot putt, etc. Stroke all putts with about the same force, except the exceptionally long ones. It is the distance of the backstroke that controls the length of the ball's roll. Let the club head do the work.
12. Keep the club head square to the line of putt, particularly on the forward stroke. The wrists do most of the work, with the left forearm sliding gently forward in a *straight* path after the ball is hit. Follow through about five inches past the original ball position. The club head *must* be *accelerating* at impact. Don't quit on the stroke.
13. Push the putter blade well through the ball, and toward the hole as indicated above.
14. For *uphill* putts, or where the grass grain is growing *toward* you, stroke more firmly.
15. For fast *downhill* putts, hold the club handle firmly, but a bit looser than for level or uphill putts. Shorten the backswing, and let the club head do the work.
16. If the slope of the green, or "break," is to the right, aim slightly to the left of the cup, increasing the aim in this manner if the break is sharp. If it is to the left, aim to the right in the same manner.
17. Don't jab the putt, but stroke *firmly*, particularly on *short putts*. Don't "baby" the putt.

SOME THINGS TO CONSIDER:

The regulation cup is 4.25 inches wide. An American ball is 1.68 inches wide.

If the ball stops even with the cup, and over one-half the ball is over the edge, the ball will drop in.

One-half the ball's diameter is .84 inches. If just a little more than one-half the ball stops at the side lip of the cup, and hangs over the side, the actual width of the target for a possible drop is not 4.25 inches, but closer to 5.75 inches. This increases the margin for error and creates a bigger target.

## How to Do It

Position ball to right of left foot.

Grip club handle at top, with hands close together.

Stand close enough to ball so that putter blade is *flat* on ground, and eye over ball.

Back of left hand and palm of right hand should face the target.

*Backstroke*

Take club head back *low* to ground, and *square* to the target (or line of the putt).

Increase or decrease the backstroke to fit the distance of putt. Keep body and head *motionless*.

Ball remains in picture to show approximate distance of club head follow-through, past the original ball position after impact.

Keep club head square to the line of target.

Wrists do most of the work, but left forearm slides gently forward after ball is stroked.

*Don't "baby" the short ones. Stroke firmly.*

## Why You Do It

In the preceding pages, outlining what to do in putting, the tips indicated are for the most part self-explanatory. Therefore we have devoted the following explanations for why you do it to general comments, instead of a cross reference to each item, as in the case of other subjects.

Anyone who has played the game of golf for any length of time knows how important good putting is to good scoring. This phase of the game accounts for one-half or more of *all* the strokes which are made in a round of golf.

Unless one learns to be a good putter, he will never score well. If he does learn to putt well, or better than average, he will win many a match game with his friends, even though a few other shots from the tee or fairway are not executed well.

The regulation number of putting strokes for an eighteen-hole round is thirty-six, or two for each hole. When this average can be reduced by several one-putt greens, it is not hard to understand the effect it can have on the scoring result.

With consistent practice, and adherence to the basic techniques which we have tried to outline, *anyone* can become a good putter.

GENERAL COMMENTS FOR WHY YOU DO IT

It is important to check the direction in which the grass grain grows before you start to make your putt—the ball will usually roll in the direction of the grain near the end of its roll.

At this same point in the roll, it will break with the lateral slope of the green's surface.

If the grain is *toward* you in your putting line, you must stroke more firmly. The same thing applies to *uphill* putts.

If it is growing *away* from you in your line, stroke a little easier, with a shorter backstroke. This also applies to *downhill* putts. Don't "baby" the putt, however. Stroke firmly enough to keep the ball on line, while using a shorter backstroke.

The grain of the grass will appear *lighter* in color when it grows *away* from you, and *darker* when it grows *toward* you.

If the green surface is *hard*, or the grass surface closely mowed, the ball will roll easier

and faster. When the grass is longer, or the surface soft or dewy, there is more resistance to the ball's roll.

Picking a spot along the line of the putt to aim at helps one to keep the putt on line, and improves concentration. It provides an objective other than the cup itself. This is important when the spot chosen is five or six inches in front of the cup, but to either side, when you are expecting a break to left or right. Without this objective, one is simply *guessing*.

When the toes of both feet are directly parallel to the putting line, there is less chance for a push to the right, or a pulled shot to the left. When playing for a *left-to-right* break, however, a slightly open stance may be used, and for a *right-to-left* break, a slightly closed stance. In the first instance, with an open stance, hit the ball near the rear of the blade. With the closed stance, strike the ball near the toe of the club face. Hitting near the rear of the blade aids the ball to fade to the right, and hitting it near the toe provides more overspin and draw to the left.

Keeping most of the weight on the left side, and back on the heels, helps keep the *body still*. Since the stroke will be to the left, there should be less chance of *moving the body with the stroke*. Some professionals advocate having the weight *even* on both feet, and some seem to have more of it on the right side. The main thing is to be *comfortable* and *relaxed*, with the head and body kept *perfectly still* during the entire stroke.

While for normal *level* ground putts the ball position at address should be slightly to the right of the left toe, this position varies for *uphill* or *downhill* putts. For *uphill* putts, play the ball more in line with the *toe* of the left foot. For *downhill* putts, play it *farther back to the right*, toward the right foot.

One should stand over the ball quite close, with the head bent down, and eye on the ball, so that the neck is parallel to the ground. This will aid in better sighting of the line, and keep the hands *close to the body* for better control of the stroke.

When one reaches out for the ball at address, it is difficult to keep the putter blade *square* to the line, in either the back or forward stroke. This could cause either a pushed or a pulled shot.

The matter of keeping the back of the left hand, and palm of the right hand facing the target helps to keep the putting stroke square to the line also. When the left hand is slightly *under* the shaft handle, it is an aid to prevent *pulling* the shot to the left. The right hand should be slightly under, and well *behind* the shaft handle for a more positive stroke forward, *square* to the line.

The "reverse overlap" grip is used by most professionals. This finds the left forefinger extended down and over the little finger, or the last two fingers of the right hand. This helps to control the hands, and again keep the stroke on line. Putting is strictly a *right-hand* push, with a left-hand guide.

Choking down on the grip, particularly for short putts, makes the club feel lighter, and often results in uncontrolled or "jerky" strokes. Gripping at the *top* of the club handle helps the putter to swing smoothly, as it should.

The distance of the backstroke generally controls and determines the distance of the roll of the ball, since the forward force of the stroke is approximately the same for most putts. For longer putts, a slightly firmer impact with the ball is generally necessary. Keep the putter blade *low to the ground in the backstroke.*

One must always be sure that the putter blade is *accelerating* at impact, and a follow-through is employed. This helps to assure a firm impact, and keeps the ball on line. To *quit* on the stroke at impact ruins the straightness of the ball's roll, and also generally leaves the ball far short of the cup.

If a forward press is employed, this is done *only with the hands, not the body, as for example, in the case of a forward press used in a tee shot.* The putting forward press helps to produce a rhythmic start of the backstroke.

Some golfers employ the "pendulum" swing, and are known as "strokers." Others use a shorter backstroke, and strike the ball more firmly. They are called "jabbers." The first use both arms and wrists, and the second, mostly the wrists. In either type of stroke the impact is not "jerky," but *smooth* and *firm.* Practice

both ways and decide for yourself which type of stroke is best suited for *your* style.

When practicing, try to sink all the putts you can from approximately *five feet,* until you feel that you can sink *all* or *most* putts from this distance. Then move back a little, and improve your accuracy for greater distances. If you will always attempt to get close enough in the first putt for an *easy* second, *some* of the first ones are bound to drop.

A main point is to keep the mind *free of doubts* or other distracting thoughts when making your putting stroke. *Think positively,* and *relax.*

You *can* be a better putter than you *think* you are!

## TO THE STUDENT

Fellow Golfers:

Since this section has been devoted to four of the most important phases of your golf game necessary for good scoring, we must continue to urge the following course of action:

1. See your school instructor, or professional teacher, for the *initial* instruction on each phase.
2. Study and *memorize* the *techniques* of each phase, and their proper *sequences* in the execution. The explanations are simply for *reference.*
3. *Practice* each phase *regularly.*
4. See your instructor for a review of your performance.
5. *Concentrate* on the *weakest* part of your game during several practice rounds of golf, until you feel you have *mastered* it.

The main purpose of this manual is to help all golfers needing instruction to have something *concise* but complete to refer to, after receiving instructions, so that none of the step-by-step techniques will be overlooked or forgotten.

Therefore, this manual may be considered as a *supplement* to the teacher's instruction.

# SECTION FIVE

# OUR LADY GOLFER

This section is devoted to a selected number of the most common errors in execution by the beginning student of the fair sex, whom we have called "our lady golfer."

With the help of the nationally known touring professional, and 1965 President of the Ladies Professional Golf Association, Barbara Romack, we have tried to show comparisons of the *right* and the *wrong* ways to execute certain phases of the game in every major division.

In the opinion of the teaching professionals whom we have consulted, as well as Miss Romack, who furnished the photo illustrations, the errors shown are those most frequently noticed by qualified instructors.

The authors hasten to point out, however, that such errors are *not* confined to students who are members of the fair sex. There are just as many male students who have equally as many errors.

More men than women play golf, although the ladies are rapidly increasing in number on courses throughout the country. In this connection, since men seem to have more opportunity to play than the women, many of them perhaps depend on the trial-and-error method of discovering their errors, and then trying to correct them.

Most of our lady golfers, however, are quite sensitive to the proficiency of their shot executions, and really take the game seriously. Perhaps that is why they are usually such good students. They are not satisfied that a thing is so; they want to know *why?*

## THIS GAME OF GOLF

### The Distaff Surge

There are several million people in the United States who play golf. In addition, there are countless thousands in foreign countries who also are devotees of the game.

An ever-increasing number of these are women, who are firmly taking their place in the time schedules of every golf course in the nation. Among them are some very fine women golfers, many of whom can give any male opponent a good run for his money.

With no disparaging intent, however, it must be acknowledged that the majority of women players (except professionals, of course) rarely score in the seventies, and only a small number of them consistently score in the eighties. The scores of most women golfers are generally in the range from 90 to 120.

To be perfectly fair, women are generally not as strong physically as men. Being the natural homemakers, their duties prevent them from playing as often as they perhaps would like to, but when they seek professional instruction, and begin to practice religiously, they are usually good students, and learn rapidly.

In addition, because of their natural grace and suppleness, most women can develop a good basic swing in a short time with the proper training. In spite of this, however, and perhaps because women are generally not quite as athletic as men, there are certain deficiencies in the form and execution of most golf shots which the average woman golfer needs to correct.

This section, therefore, is devoted principally to the corrections and adjustments necessary to aid in reducing the scores of "our lady golfer."

## THE TEE SHOT

No. 1 Wood

### Do's and Don'ts

The following right (R) and wrong (W) comparisons, shown under subheadings, cover the major problems in the tee shots.

### STANCE AND ADDRESS

1. (W) Standing too stiff and erect while addressing the ball.

   (R) "Sit down to the ball," with knees fixed, and posterior protruding slightly. (This is not unladylike on the golf course.) Also, bend the upper body and head forward about thirty degrees, but with weight firmly on *both heels and soles* of the feet.

### BACKSWING

2. (W) Lifting club head sharply at start of backswing.

   (R) Start backswing *low* and *slow*, dragging club head *close to ground* for first twelve to twenty-four inches. Swivel hips to right, but keep head over ball.

3. (W) Swaying hips laterally to right on backswing, instead of *pivoting*. Lifting left heel too high off the ground.

   (R) At start of backswing, swivel the hips to the right, and keep the head bent and still. Left knee *dips* to right, and weight shifts to *inside* of right foot.

4. (W) Allowing left arm to bend or collapse on the backswing.

   (R) Start backswing with both arms *fully extended,* and with *left arm* and *club shaft* forming a *straight* line. For the balance of the backswing, keep left arm comfortably straight (not stiff).

5. (W) Allowing hands to loosen and "roll" on the grip at the top of the backswing.

   (R) At the top of the backswing, the club shaft should point in a straight line over the shoulders toward the target. Keep hands firm on the club grip, but don't allow wrists to become "sloppy" (flexed). Loosening the grip on the club handle changes the position of the club face on the downswing, and at impact with the ball.

6. (W) Swaying hips laterally to the left on downswing, with weight still on right foot (lunging at the ball).

   (R) Start downswing with a slight lateral slide to the left, followed by rotation or swivel of the hips to the left, which shifts the weight to the left also.

7. (W) Flipping the club head at the ball on downswing, and at impact.

   (R) Keep left arm fully extended, and hit *through* the ball, not *at* it. "Throw" the club head out toward the target, with *full* follow-through.

## Illustrations

**RIGHT**
"Sit down to the ball," with knees flexed, and posterior protruding slightly.

**WRONG**
Standing too stiff and erect while addressing the ball.

**RIGHT**

After starting backswing *low* and *slow,* with both arms fully extended, cock wrists at about hip level.

Swivel hips to right and dip left knee to right, while dropping left shoulder under chin.

**WRONG**
Swaying hips laterally to right.

**RIGHT**

On downswing, lead with hips first, then
shoulders, then arms and hands. Follow through
completely.

**WRONG**
Don't sway hips laterally to left, with weight
still on right foot.

## Analysis

In Section One, "The Basic Swing," a complete explanation of all the techniques is given under "Why You Do It" for the grip, stance and address, backswing, downswing, and impact and follow-through.

The following pinpoints the reasons for the right (R) and wrong (W) comparisons on the preceding pages.

## STANCE AND ADDRESS

### ITEM 1.

(W) When the body is too stiff and erect at address, it is not possible to pivot properly in either the backswing or the downswing. The shoulders cannot tilt as they should, the swing is flat, and body sway and loss of balance just cannot be prevented. Moreover, with such a stance the swing will be made with the arms alone, with consequent loss of power in the hit, if by some miracle the ball is *hit at all*.

(R) As the illustrating photos indicate, all these errors are eliminated with the proper stance, backswing, and downswing. The body, while not rigidly erect, remains almost vertical, as though pivoting in a barrel or cylinder, with *no sway*, and with the *head kept still*.

## BACKSWING

### ITEM 2.

(W) Lifting the club head sharply curtails the length of the swing arc, and contributes to lateral sway to the right in the backswing. In addition, proper pivoting of the body is inhibited, preventing the coiling of the right side, for release later in the downswing for added power in the hit. Result: you just chop at the ball.

(R) The backswing is started by a push of the left arm to the right, with both arms fully extended, and the left arm in a perfectly straight line with the club shaft. The club head is kept *close to the ground* for the first twelve to twenty-four inches; then it begins to rise through the proper pivoting of the body to the right.

As the hips swivel to the right, the left knee also dips forward in this direction. The left shoulder tilts down and under the chin, with the head *kept still*, and *eye on the ball*, until the player's back faces the target. The cocking of the wrists takes place automatically as the turn to the right is completed. Now the right side of the body is *coiled* for *power*.

### ITEM 3.

(W) The above explanations have already covered the matter of lateral sway, and the lack of proper pivoting. One of the major factors which contribute to these errors, however, is lifting the left heel too high off the ground. *Keep it down*, with very little heel lift.

(R) No need to say more on this subject than is already covered in Item 2.

### ITEM 4.

(W) Allowing the left arm to bend or collapse on the backswing is one of the main causes of picking up the club head sharply. This again reduces the plane of the swing arc, and causes one to chop at the ball in the downswing, instead of *swinging through*.

(R) This subject is also covered in Item 2.

### ITEM 5.

(W) When the hands loosen and "roll" on the grip at the top of the backswing, the alignment of the club face is changed, and it is difficult if not impossible to regrip and square the alignment again for a clean solid hit on the downswing.

(R) When the club is taken back too far, allowing the club head to dip below a horizontal level over the shoulders, it is difficult to prevent a loosening of the grip, and undue flexing of the wrists. Keep the backswing compact, and in one piece.

Even though the club may not be taken back as far as some players are able, this slight difference will not penalize one in the power of the hit as much as overswinging would spoil timing. Keep a firm grip with the last three fingers of the left hand, particularly the little finger.

## DOWNSWING

### ITEM 6.

(W) When the hips are allowed to sway laterally to the left, with the weight still on the right foot, it is not possible to hit through the ball and attain any appreciable distance in the flight. All one usually does is lunge at the ball through this procedure, with a resulting scuffed shot or "fat" hit.

(R) Actually, before starting to bring the club into the downswing there should be a slight lateral *slide* of the hips to the left, transferring the weight to the left side. This is followed by a rotation of the hips to the left. Then the shoulders turn to the left, which causes the arms and hands to move into the downswing.

### ITEM 7.

(W) When the club head is flipped at the ball, instead of hitting *through* it, only the weakest kind of impact is possible, with resulting loss of distance as well as flight direction.

(R) At impact, the left arm should be fully extended, and the right arm *slightly bent.* By hitting through the ball with the club head going out straight toward the target, the left hand and arm retain control of the swing, allowing the power of the right hand to be fully utilized without overtaking the left.

A full follow-through is therefore set up, causing the ball to "ride" on the club face after the initial compression from the hit, instead of just *popping* the ball weakly when the club head is merely flipped at the ball.

ADVICE TO "OUR LADY GOLFER":

There is no denying that learning to swing the wood clubs is more difficult than swinging the shorter irons. The swing arc is longer, and one swings harder with the woods in order to attain the maximum distance from the hit.

However, our lady golfer should not become discouraged when she begins to swing these clubs, because sooner or later her natural grace and suppleness will help establish good timing. This coupled with the instruction in the technique of the entire swing which her school instructor or PGA teaching professional can provide, should accomplish the desired results in a relatively short time.

Resolve to take lessons *regularly,* until you have mastered the swing with your wood clubs. Then experience the thrill when your drives off the tee match those of *most* of the men players. Want to bet?

## THE FAIRWAY WOODS

### Do's and Don'ts

The major problems, showing right (R) and wrong (W) executions.

1. (W) Stance too wide, body too upright and stiff.

   (R) As for tee shots, feet should be spread about the width of the shoulders, and with weight on both *heels* and soles of the feet. Flex knees, protrude posterior, and bend upper body and head forward about thirty degrees.

2. (W) Hands too far to *left* on grip. (Weak grip.)

   (R) Use "hooker's grip," with both hands moved more to *right*. This overcomes tendency to slice, and helps to produce more distance.

3. (W) Playing the ball too far to right of stance.

(R) For the No. 2 wood, play the ball off the *left* heel (for level lies) to make impact at the *bottom* of the swing arc. For the Nos. 3 and 4 woods, play the ball approximately *two inches* to the *right* of *left heel,* to make impact with the ball just *before* the bottom of the swing arc. For uphill and downhill lies, play the ball off the "high" foot.

4. (W) Lunging at the ball with weight on right foot on downswing. Trying to scoop the ball up.

(R) Lead downswing with hips first, then full shoulder turn, then "pull down" with the hands and arms, with wrists *still cocked* until at hip level. *Shift weight to left foot.*

5. (W) Waving club head at the ball. No "punch."

(R) While maintaining good timing and balance, *hit hard* and *through* the ball, not *at* it. Follow through completely, with fully extended arms, and finish with the hands high.

For attaining the extra distance, which women in general need, the fairway wood is the club to use. *Concentrate* on all shots with these clubs, and have *confidence.* There is nothing to fear if your swing is right and the ball is positioned properly.

One of the most important things to remember in making successful fairway wood shots is *ball position* at address. For the No. 2 wood, by playing the ball off the *left heel,* and with impact made at the *bottom* of the swing arc, you *sweep* the ball off the ground. With the shorter Nos. 3 and 4 woods, impact is made just *before* the bottom of the swing arc, and only a small divot is taken.

**Illustrations**

RIGHT

Stance and ball position for level fairway lie. Feet spread about the width of shoulders. Left arm and club shaft form a straight line from shoulder to club head.

**RIGHT**
Showing "hooker's grip," with both hands turned more to right on club handle.

**WRONG**
Stance too wide. Body too upright and stiff.

**WRONG**
(For most women)
Showing weak grip with both hands turned more to left.

**RIGHT**

Showing hips leading downswing, and with
arms being drawn down, with wrists still cocked
at hip level.

**WRONG**
Waving club head at the ball. Rolling the wrists.
No "punch," and no follow-through.

## Analysis

The following explanations offer some of the reasons for the right (R) and wrong (W) comparisons on the preceding pages. For more complete coverage see Section Two.

### ITEM 1.

(W) When the stance is too wide, and the body too stiff and erect, proper pivoting of the hips is inhibited, and the desired plane of the swing arc is restricted. It is *flat!* As a result, there is a tendency to "come off the ball" with a topped shot, or at best a "punched" hit with very little trajectory to the flight, and poor distance.

(R) The stance for normal fairway shots should be similar to that for shots off the tee, except that it is a trifle closer to the ball because of shorter shafts for the Nos. 2, 3, and 4 woods. Note the photo illustration for the *right* stance. The knees are slightly flexed, allowing for an easy pivot, and the upper body and head inclined. This is the position for staying down to the ball, which is vitally necessary for good swing execution.

### ITEM 2.

(W) Placing the hands on the grip too far to the left creates a weak grip, which most often results in a sliced shot and loss of distance.

(R) Most women (amateurs, of course) need all the distance they can achieve, particularly when using woods. By moving the hands on the grip more to the *right,* a "hooker's grip" is created, generally helping to accomplish more distance in the hit. Assuming the rest of the swing is correct, this type of grip helps provide more overspin to the ball, and even a slight draw from right to left in the ball's flight, all of which aids in attaining the distance desired.

### ITEM 3.

(W) Playing the ball too far to the right of the stance causes the impact to be made *considerably before* the bottom of the swing arc has been reached. This usually creates a very low trajectory in the flight of the ball with resulting loss of distance. When hitting into a strong headwind, it is well to play the ball back toward the center of the stance in order to keep the flight low. For the same reason, a low flight can be expected *whenever* the ball is played from this position, with resulting loss of distance.

(R) The correct ball position in relation to the stance when playing fairway woods is clearly shown under Item 3 of a preceding page under the subject of Do's and Don'ts. By playing the ball forward (closer to the left foot as indicated) for all *level* lies, a higher trajectory and greater distance of the ball's flight is generally assured. The exceptions to such ball positions occur when playing a *downhill* lie, or when hitting into a strong headwind. In such instances, the ball should be played closer to the center of the stance, or even the right foot in order to keep the flight of the ball low. Proper positioning of the ball is one of the most important factors in making good wood shots from the fairway.

### ITEM 4.

(W) "Lunging" at the ball with the weight still on the right foot generally results in *scuffing* the shot, particularly when trying to scoop the ball up.

(R) As for tee shots, the start of the downswing begins with a slight slide of the hips to the left, followed by their full rotation, which braces the left side. (Make sure, in this bracing process, that the left knee is flexed, and the left leg is not straight and stiff.) Then as the shoulders turn to the left, this causes the arms and hands to be drawn down. In this process the tip of the club handle should be pointing to the ground, with the wrists still *cocked,* and the left arm straight. Then the right elbow returns *close* to the right side as the hands reach hip level. Now the wrists *uncock,* snapping the club head through the ball for a strong, solid impact.

ITEM 5.

(W) As the illustrating photo shows, waving the club head at the ball fails to accomplish anything except a *weak hit* for only a few yards, and not a very straight shot at that. Note the rolling of the wrists, with the right hand completely overtaking the left, and with the club head finishing to the *left rear* of the player.

(R) Swing *smoothly,* using the swing technique described in Item 4. For fairway wood shots, *hit hard without lunging.* Hit through the ball with full follow-through, and finish with the hands high.

## IRON PLAY

### Do's and Don'ts

Playing the *irons,* and the right (R) and wrong (W) ways to use them.

1. (W) Taking stance with feet spread too far apart, and too far from the ball.

   (R) Iron shots, particularly the short irons, require a more "upright" arc to the swing than do the wood clubs. Narrow the stance, and stand *closer* to the ball, keeping the sole of the club head flat when grounded.

2. (W) Grip too loose, causing the club face to open up with the shock of impact with the ball and ground. Wrong placement of hands on grip.

   (R) Grip the club *firmly* but not *tensely* in *left* hand, with the back of left hand facing the target. Place the right hand on club grip so that the *palm faces the target also.*

3. (W) Lifting club head sharply at start of backswing. Bending left arm.

   (R) Start backswing *low* and *slow,* with both arms fully extended. Keep left arm straight but not stiff.

4. (W) Failing to cock and uncock the wrists. Waving the club back, with arms too stiff, and swinging downward with the arms alone.

   (R) Cock the wrists at about hip level in the backswing, and uncock them at about the same point on the downswing, with the left arm straight, and the right elbow moving in front and close to the right hip. Hit the ball on the *downswing.* Don't try to scoop it up.

5. (W) Rolling the wrists to the left at impact with the ball.

   (R) Swing club head through the ball, and out, straight toward the target, with the *back* of the *left* hand, and the *palm* of the *right* hand facing the target also. Don't lose control with the left hand, or allow the right hand to overtake it.

6. (W) Flipping the club head at the ball. *Quitting* on the shot.

   (R) Follow through *low* and *completely.* Finish with the hands high.

## Illustrations

**RIGHT**

Proper stance, narrower and closer to ball than for wood clubs.

Palm of right hand and back of left hand facing the target.

**WRONG**

Stance too wide, and too far from the ball.

**RIGHT**

Showing arms extended, with wrists beginning to cock at about hip level.

Very little hip turn, but full shoulder turn about to take place as backswing progresses.

**WRONG**

Lifting club head sharply, with *no turn.*

**RIGHT**

Club head being stroked through the ball, and out toward the target, with fully extended arms.

**WRONG**

Flipping the club head at the ball, and rolling the wrists. Quitting on the shot. *"No punch."*

## Analysis

On the preceding pages, comparisons of the right and wrong ways to execute iron shots are shown. The following give the reasons for each item.

### ITEM 1.

(W) When the stance is too wide, proper pivoting of the body is restricted, and the swing becomes too flat. In addition, when one stands too far from the ball, the club head usually rests on its heel, preventing a square impact of the club face with the ball. Generally this results in inaccurate flight direction.

(R) Because the shafts of the iron clubs are shorter than the wood clubs, one should stand closer to the ball. The correct distance is indicated when the sole of the club head is *flat* on the ground at address. Also, since the backswing is shorter, and more vertical for iron shots, the stance should be narrower, as indicated in the illustration. With the knees flexed, this permits a proper body pivot for a compact, one-piece backswing.

### ITEM 2.

(W) A loose grip generally does two things that cause trouble. First, it causes "floating" hands and wrists at the top of the backswing, which changes the club face alignment. This in turn prevents a square, solid impact with the ball on the downswing. Second, when the impact is made, the shock of contact with the ball and then the ground usually opens up the club face, resulting in a *sliced* hit.

(R) The club handle should be gripped firmly with the left hand, particularly with the *last three fingers*, and with the back of the left hand and palm of the right hand facing the target. The hands should be slightly *ahead* of the ball at address, *and* at impact with the ball.

### ITEM 3.

(W) Lifting the club head sharply, and bending the left arm, at the start of the backswing, shortens the swing arc and causes one to simply chop at the ball on the downswing. Result; neither distance nor good direction of the shot is possible. In addition, the shot will doubtless be *scuffed* or *topped*.

(R) Even though the backswing is shorter, and more vertical with the iron clubs, the *start* of the backswing should be made by taking the club head back *low to the ground* with fully extended arms. The left arm remains comfortably straight throughout the entire swing. This arm controls the entire swing plane, and by keeping it straight it is able to guide the club down and *through* the ball for a clean, solid impact.

### ITEM 4.

(W) When you fail to cock and uncock the wrists during the backswing and downswing, what else can you do but just wave the club back and forth stiffly with the arms alone. This would be like using a croquet mallet, because if the ball is hit at all it probably would just *skim* over the ground for a short distance. In addition, should the player lift her head, or try to scoop the ball up with the weight still on the right foot, it is possible the club head will pass *over* the top of the ball and *miss it entirely*.

(R) The wrists should cock at about hip level on the backswing, and uncock at about the same point on the downswing, with the left arm kept straight throughout the entire swing. As the right elbow moves in close to the right side on the downswing, the wrists begin to uncock, snapping the club head down and through the ball. Since the impact is made *just before* the bottom of the swing arc is reached, this causes the back of the ball to be hit first, then a divot taken under the ball. This impact lifts the ball with the proper backspin, which causes it to rise, and keeps the flight straight on line. When one tries to scoop the ball up, a *fat* hit or a *skulled* shot generally results.

ITEM 5.

(W) Rolling of the wrists to the left at impact with the ball means that the right hand has overtaken and passed the left. This *closes* the club face, and always results in a pulled shot to the left, which often ends up in trouble. Obviously, in the process, the club head finishes to the left of the target line.

(R) The left hand and arm should always be in control in every shot, with the back of this hand and the palm of the right hand facing the target at impact. When this is done the club face will be *square* to the target at impact, and will enable you to hit through the ball, with the club head going out straight to the objective. Accordingly, there is only one direction for the *ball* to go—*straight also.*

ITEM 6.

(W) When you flip the club head at the ball and *quit* on the shot, only a weak hit is possible. This flipping action is usually accompanied by a rolling of the wrists, as indicated in the illustration. With the club head finishing to the left rear of the player, a straight shot is impossible.

(R) The contrasting illustration shows the proper follow-through, *low* and *complete,* with fully extended arms. Note the club head pointing straight out at the target, with the back of the left hand and palm of the right hand also facing the objective. As the follow-through is completed, the body turns until it too faces the target, and the hands raise as the swing is completed.

TIPS ON IRON PLAY

1. Iron clubs are used for *accuracy,* not extra distance.

2. Swing with only 80 percent of your power. *Don't slug* with irons.

3. *Don't underclub.* When in doubt, use an extra club length.

4. Grip the club *firmly,* but not tensely.

5. Keep the hands *ahead* of the ball at address, and at impact.

6. Keep the back of the left hand and palm of the right hand *facing the target.*

7. Keep the left arm straight, and hit *through* the ball, not *at* it.

8. Follow through *low* and *completely,* throwing the club head out straight toward the target.

9. Take lessons regularly from a good instructor, then *practice—practice—practice.*

## THE SHORT-SHORT GAME

### Do's and Don'ts

These are delicate shots, but ones easily mastered with practice. Shown below are a few examples of the wrong (W) and the right (R) ways to make them.

**PITCHING**

1. (W) Keeping weight on *right* foot, and using too much body turn. Result: fat hit, or scuffed shot.

   (R) Keep at least 60 percent of weight on *left* foot, with both feet even on *heels* and soles. Swing mostly with arms and wrist action.

2. (W) Quitting on the shot. Stubbing club head into the ground.

(R) Take a smooth, slow backswing. On the downswing, stroke firmly and *through* the ball, taking divot. Follow through with straight left arm, and with club head facing the target at the finish. *Don't scoop this shot.*

## CHIPPING

1. (W) Topping or sculling the shot.

(R) Don't try to scoop or lift the ball. Let the loft of the club face do this. Keep weight on the *left* foot, and keep the body *still.*
At address, and throughout the stroke, keep the hands *ahead* of the ball. Take the club head back *low* to the ground.
On the downstroke, lead the club head down and *through* the ball, with *straight left arm and wrist.*
Make solid, crisp contact with the ball. *Bump* it!

## SAND TRAP PLAY

1. (W) Failing to get the ball out. *Stubbing* club head in the sand.

(R) Open the club face and stance, playing the ball off the *left* foot. This assumes that the ball is sitting up well on the sand.
Take club back to the outside of the flight line, with sharply upright backswing, and with early wrist break. On the downswing, cut *under* and across the ball from the *outside in,* striking the *sand* approximately *one* to *two inches behind* the ball.
*Follow through completely,* and finish with the hands fairly high. *Swing firmly but smoothly.*

**Illustrations**

RIGHT

For the short pitch, keep hands *ahead* of ball at address, and at impact. Weight is mostly on the left foot.

**RIGHT**
Stance and address for chip shot showing hands *ahead* of ball with weight even on both feet.

**WRONG**
Scooping the shot with hands *behind* the ball at impact, and rolling the wrists.

**WRONG**
Showing hands *behind* ball at impact. Note club head striking ball in the middle, resulting in a sculled shot. Also, weight appears to be mostly on right foot.

RIGHT
Showing complete follow-through after impact with sand *under* the ball.

**WRONG**

Stubbing club head into the sand at impact.
Only a miracle could get the ball up and out
this way.

## Analysis

More complete coverage of these subjects can be found in Section Four. The following give a few reasons for the comparisons on the preceding pages.

### PITCHING

#### ITEM 1.

(W) Besides the possible fat hits, or scuffed shots, resulting from the weight being kept on the right foot, and using too much body turn, there is the additional danger of swinging the body around to the left, causing the shot to be pulled in that direction.

(R) The short pitch shot involves *no turn of the body at all*. It should be made mostly with the arms, and with wrist action. The backstroke is short and quite upright, since *accuracy* is the real objective, not distance. Most of the weight should be kept on the left side throughout the entire short swing. The only body action should be a rolling of the *left knee* to the *right* on the *backstroke*, and the same roll of the *right knee* to the *left* on the *downstroke*.

#### ITEM 2.

(W) When you *quit* on the short pitch shot by stubbing the club head into the ground behind the ball, all you do is to punch the ball, which often results in "sculling" it (hitting the ball at a point near the center or top, with the bottom edge, or sole of the club head). There is generally no loft to the shot, or certainty of direction, or distance. The ball generally just scoots across the ground.

(R) The backstroke should be smooth and "lazy." The downswing should be firm and *crisp*. Keep the hands *ahead* of the ball, and stroke *through* it with a straight left arm. If the follow-through is *low* and *complete*, with the club head going out in the direction of the target, there is only one place for the ball to go —*straight* to the target also.

### CHIPPING

#### ITEM 1.

(W) Topping or sculling the chip shot is generally caused by one of two errors. First, by taking the eye off the ball at the point of impact (by being too anxious to see where the ball is going before it is hit), and second, by trying to *scoop* the ball off the ground.

(R) As indicated on the preceding pages, keep the *body still* with the *weight on the left side*, and the hands *ahead* of the ball. Take the club head back low to the ground for only a short distance. Then lead the club head *down* and *through* the ball *crisply* with a straight left arm and wrist. "Bump" the ball, with *lots of right-hand action*, letting the loft of the club head do the lifting. (Don't scoop this shot.) It is actually an exaggerated putt.

### SAND TRAP PLAY

#### ITEM 1.

(W) When one just "punches" at the ball, stubbing the club head into the sand, and finishing with it buried behind the ball, there is hardly any chance of getting it out of the trap.

(R) There are several techniques in making shots out of a sand trap, depending upon the texture and condition of the sand (wet or dry, fluffy or heavy) and whether the ball is sitting up well on the sand, or if it is buried. Other things to consider are the height of the trap lip in front of the ball, how close to the lip the ball is resting, the distance to the flag stick, and how close the stick is to the near edge of the green.

All of these factors play a part in determining how close to the ball one must strike the sand with the club head, and if the club head should be open, closed, or "hooded." Another point is the amount of force one should apply to the stroke.

All of these points are adequately covered in Section Four, "The Short-Short Game," and are worth the effort it takes to study and practice them.

For purposes of this comparison, the preceding pages cover the technique when the ball is *sitting up well* on the sand. One of the main points to remember is to swing *smoothly* and *firmly*, and *follow through completely*. With a little earnest practice, and adherence to the proper techniques, one can learn to be a good trap shot player in a very short time.

**Illustrations**

## PUTTING ERRORS

### Do's and Don'ts

There are several different styles and strokes used in putting by various people, so use the one which gets the best results for *you*.

Here are a few common errors (E) and their corrections (C).

1. (E) Putting off line.

   (C) Sight the line of putt carefully, from in back of the ball, which should be played slightly to the *right* of the toe of the *left* foot. Grip the club with the back of the left hand turned slightly *left* of being square to the line of the putt, and the right hand slightly *under* the club handle, with the palm square to the line.
   Stroke the ball firmly, with *club face square to the line,* and with complete follow-through.

2. (E) Ball stops *short* of the hole.

   (C) Don't "baby" the stroke. Stroke firmly, particularly on uphill putts. Check for grass grain growing *against* the line of the putt.

3. (E) Ball runs *past* the hole.

   (C) Pick a spot on the green approximately six inches in front of the hole to aim your putt. Gauge your putt to reach this spot, and to roll in to the cup from that point. Where there is a slope to the green (left to right or right to left), estimate the amount of the break and choose a similar spot slightly in front of the hole, but to either side, to which you will aim your putt.

4. (E) Pushed or pulled shots.

   (C) Keep stroke *square* to the line at *impact,* and follow through at least five inches past the original ball position at address.

RIGHT

Showing proper stance and ball position.

Keep body *still,* and eye directly over the ball, with back of left hand and palm of right hand facing the target.

WRONG

Ball positioned too far forward, with hands behind the ball at address. This frequently results in a pulled shot to the left.

**RIGHT**
Showing a firm stroke *square* to the line.
Also, the left arm has moved slightly forward
from the original position at address.

**WRONG**
Flipping club head at the ball with improper
control of wrists and left arm.

This almost always results in the ball running
past the cup.

**RIGHT**
Stroke the putt firmly, especially the *short* putts. *Don't "baby" them.*

**WRONG**
Showing a pulled shot to left, caused mainly by improper hand position, and failure to keep putter blade *square* to the line of putt.

## Analysis

### ITEM 1.

(E) Putting off line is to be expected at times by all golfers, even the best. To try to reduce such instances to a minimum is the best anyone can do. There are many factors which often contribute to misalignment of the putt, such as the contour of the green and the direction of the grass grain. The pros, however, learn to "read" the greens with considerable accuracy, and so can you!

(C) The preceding pages cover a few of the points to consider. For more complete coverage of this subject, see Section Four, "The Short-Short Game."

### ITEM 2.

(E) When the ball stops short of the hole the cause can be any number of things—e.g., stubbing the stroke or "babying" it, not stroking firmly enough, particularly for uphill putts, or the roll of the ball may be slowed due to the grass grain growing *against* the line of the putt. In essence, the length of the backstroke mostly controls the distance the ball will roll, except for the factors mentioned above. Another exception is when one uses a short "jabbing" stroke, which is not always easy to control.

(C) If you are what is known as a "stroker," one method of gauging the distance of the backstroke for various length putts is as follows: Take a stance square to the line of the putt with feet close together. Then move the right foot one width to the right, and take the putter blade back to the outside of the right foot for a *ten-foot putt*. Move the right foot one more width for a *twenty-foot putt*, taking the putter blade back to the outside of the right foot in the same manner. Increase the distance of the backstroke correspondingly for longer putts. In using this method of gauging distance, remember that the force of the forward stroke should be quite similar for all putts. Only the length of the backstroke varies.

### ITEM 3.

(E) When the ball runs *past* the hole, it is often due to the condition of the green, in cases where it is hard and "fast," or it can be due to stroking the ball too hard. This is particularly true for *downhill* putts, where the length of the backstroke and the force of the forward stroke must be curtailed.

(C) While we agree that there is some merit to the statement, "never up, never in," there is also considerable danger of running so far past the hole that the next putt is also missed. Another point is that if the ball hits the cup square, but is too fast, it seldom drops in, particularly if the back of the cup is lower than the front, as in the case of a downhill putt.

Try picking a spot about six inches in front of the cup to which you will aim instead of the cup itself. If there is a slope to the right or left near the cup, play the break by picking a spot to the right or left front of the cup, from which the ball will fade to the hole.

### ITEM 4.

(E) Most pushed (to the right) or pulled (to the left) putts are due to not keeping the putter blade *square* to the line of the putt, particularly in the forward stroke. These errors, however, can also be due to an improper stance when addressing the ball, which also may not be square to the line.

(C) Make sure that the feet are *squarely* at *right angles* to the putting line, unless there is a break from *right to left*, were a slightly *closed* stance may be used (left foot a little ahead of the right). If the break is from *left to right*, a slightly open stance is helpful (right foot a little ahead of the left). Actually since you are playing the break in either case, and aiming in front, and to the right or left of the cup, the closed or open stance will also be *square* to the spot you are aiming for. It is just that simple!

Only through *practice* can one develop the finesse to be a good putter.

## DISTANCE CHART

### For Women

As for men, the distance attained by the use of various clubs will differ, depending upon several factors, such as the player's age, size, strength, and skill, as well as wind direction and velocity, and damp air.

The chart below shows the average distances to be expected under normal conditions for average amateur women players.

Check your own distances, and record them in the space provided. Then choose the club which will get the best results for *you*. *Don't underclub.*

TIPS TO REMEMBER

1. You will generally attain more distance when you are fresh and relaxed.
2. Don't *press*. Swing smoothly, and with good timing.
3. For wood shots, *hit hard, but swing smoothly. Don't lunge at the ball.*
4. For iron shots, *swing with only about 80 percent of your power. Iron shots are for direction*, not extra distance.
5. When in doubt, use an *extra* club length to reach your target. *Bury your pride.* The main thing is to *get there!*

GOOD LUCK

| CLUB | AVERAGE DISTANCE | YOUR DISTANCE |
|------|------------------|---------------|
| No. 1 Wood | 180 Yards | ----- |
| No. 2 " | 170 " | ----- |
| No. 3 " | 160 " | ----- |
| No. 4 " | 150 " | ----- |
| No. 5 " | 140 " | ----- |
| No. 2 Iron | 150 " | ----- |
| No. 3 " | 140 " | ----- |
| No. 4 " | 130 " | ----- |
| No. 5 " | 120 " | ----- |
| No. 6 " | 110 " | ----- |
| No. 7 " | 100 " | ----- |
| No. 8 " | 90 " | ----- |
| No. 9 " | 80 " | ----- |
| Wedge | 50 " | ----- |

# SECTION SIX

SECTION SIX

# PROFESSIONAL TIPS

HOW TO IMPROVE YOUR SCORE

This section is devoted to the ways and means of getting you out of trouble. In every practice round, or in tournament competition, every player is faced with situations which call for the utmost in careful execution of the most delicate shots possible.

The following is a listing of most of these shots, and suggestions for correcting some of the more common errors of amateur players:

"This Game of Golf"—Your Real Opponent, the Golf Course.
Corrections: Topping, Scuffing, Skying
Corrections: Slicing, Hooking, Shanking
Playing the Wind
Rainy Day Play
Intentional Hook or Slice
Intentional High or Low Ball
Side Hill Lies (ball above or below feet)
Sand Trap Shots
Trouble Shots
Hard Ground Lies, Frozen Ground Lies, Punch Shots, Pitching from Grassy Banks

This is the section to refer to for problems experienced in your practice rounds. A quick inspection of the proper procedure to follow may save you strokes.

## THIS GAME OF GOLF

Your Real Opponent, the Golf Course

In the preceding sections we have attempted to provide the basic techniques if one is to make any appreciable progress in learning golf.

These are not hard to learn, provided the student first seeks professional instruction, and then is willing to *study* and *practice* what has been taught. There is no other way.

Now we come to corrections for various stroking errors (faults experienced by all golfers, even the best, from time to time) and abnormal lies. Playing the wind, rainy day play, and other abnormal shots are frequently faced by all golfers.

There is considerable doubt whether anyone, beginner or the more experienced player, ever attains the maximum in perfection for all the shots he is called upon to make. If he did his performance would become monotonous, and there would be no challenge.

This is the main reason most people love the game once they have tried it. The longer they play, the more this feeling grows. There is just no game like it, bar none.

It is the only game where your opponent is *yourself*. Any mistakes which are made are yours alone. They are not dependent on what someone else does.

Many players have the idea that they are playing some other person as their opponent. To a degree that they want to achieve a lower score, they are. If one is careful to make as few mistakes as possible, and his playing companion does not use the same care, however, sooner or later the one with less mistakes will come out ahead.

So play your *real* opponent, *the golf course*, and learn the shots which will help you to beat it.

This section is designed as a supplement to the instruction which should first be obtained from your PGA teaching professional or school instructor. These are his *professional tips*.

## CORRECTIONS

### FOR TOPPING

1. Stand closer to the ball.
2. Keep *head still* throughout the swing. Keep *eye on the ball*.
3. Concentrate on swinging smoothly, not on looking up to see where the ball goes.
4. Don't stiffen or lock right knee on the backswing.
5. Make sure the weight is shifted to the right leg during the backswing, but be sure to *shift full weight to the left foot on the downswing*.
6. Don't try to lift the ball into the air with body action, or a flick of the wrists.

### FOR SCUFFING

1. Don't try to "kill" the ball. Swing smoothly.
2. Don't bend the left knee too much on the backswing.
3. Keep arms *fully extended* at the start of the backswing.
4. Don't allow the right side of the body to sag.
5. *Shift the weight completely to the left on the downswing.*

Fat hits are mainly caused by failing to shift the weight to the left foot on the downswing.

### FOR SKYING

1. Tee the ball off the *left instep* for driving off the tee, so that impact is made just after the *bottom* of the *swing arc has been reached*, and at the *start* of the upswing.
2. Don't lift the club head sharply on the backswing. Keep it *low to the ground* for the first twelve to twenty-four inches.
3. Don't chop down at the ball.
4. Don't roll the wrists.

### FOR SLICING

1. Grip the club so that at least two or three knuckles of the left hand are showing.
2. Use a square or slightly closed stance.
3. Start the backswing *low* and *slow*. Keep the right elbow close to the body until the top of the backswing.
4. Do not break the wrists until the hands reach hip height.
5. Keep a *firm* grip on the club handle.
6. On the downswing, don't *reach* for the ball, but swing from inside out.

### FOR HOOKING

1. Grip the club with both hands placed more to the *left* than customarily. Only one or two knuckles of the left hand should show.
2. Start the backswing with the left hand in control, and maintain this control throughout the entire swing.
3. Do not roll the wrists.
4. At the top of the backswing, make sure that the right wrist is *under* the club handle.
5. On the downswing, don't let the right hand dominate.

### FOR SHANKING    (hitting the ball on the hosel of the shaft)

1. Stand farther from the ball at address.
2. Keep the weight even, on both soles and *heels* of the feet. Don't lurch forward.
3. Keep right elbow close to the body on the downswing.

4. Don't *reach* for the ball, or swing across it from outside in.
5. Keep the right shoulder *behind* the ball.

## PLAYING THE WIND

### HEADWIND

1. Play the ball more toward the right foot than usual.
2. Use *two* club lengths *more* than usual.
3. When using iron clubs, grip the club *shorter* on the shaft handle, and use a punch shot. (This means using a restricted backswing and restricted follow-through.)
4. For required longer shots off the fairway, use a driver (No. 1 wood), provided the ball is *sitting up well* on the grass.
5. Don't expect or depend on reaching the greens in the regulation number of strokes when hitting against a headwind. Plan your strategy for the shots to follow, to compensate for any possible loss of distance.
6. When pitching to greens, "hood" the club face more to facilitate a lower flight of the ball.
7. Check the velocity and direction of the wind by tossing wisps of grass. Also check the wind direction of the flag on the green, as well as the movement of tree branches near the target.
8. Swing *smoothly*. Don't try to *overpower* the wind.

### DOWNWIND

1. Tee the ball higher (but not too high).
2. Play the ball off the *left* instep.
3. Use *one* club length *less* than usual.
4. On short iron shots, don't pitch *to* the flag stick. Aim short of the stick for the ball to run up to the target (particularly where the green slopes downhill in line to the cup). Play the pitch shot closer to the flag stick where the line to the cup is *uphill*.
5. Use a *chip* shot when just off the green.

### CROSSWIND

1. Use *one* club length *more* than usual.
2. For *right-to-left* wind, hit the ball to the *right* of the target.
3. For *left-to-right* wind, hit the ball to the *left* of the target.
4. Keep the swing smooth, and in one piece.

## RAINY DAY PLAY

1. Keep the club grips dry. Wipe the handles and the club heads with a towel after each shot.
2. Use *one* club length *more* than usual for all *full* shots. In wet weather the air is heavier, which reduces the distance of the ball's flight.
3. Hit the ball *cleanly*. Try to "sweep" the ball off the ground wherever possible. The club head has a tendency to dig too deep into soggy ground. Also, wet grass between the club face and the ball, could spoil the shot.
4. Lift away from "casual water." This is O.K. under U.S.G.A. rules.
5. For pitch shots, aim as close to the target as possible. Wet greens or casual water restrict the ball's run up to the cup.
6. Use a chip shot or putt the ball out of sand traps wherever possible. A sand wedge will usually bounce off wet sand unless played perfectly.
7. When just off the edge of the green don't try to chip, or run the ball up to the target. (Pitch it.) Casual water or heavy, wet greens slow down the roll of the ball.
8. Play the ball off the left toe, and stroke a putt more firmly than usual, particularly on uphill putts.
9. See your pro shop for rain clothes, umbrellas, and towels. These articles can be carried in your golf bag, and are life savers when you are caught in a sudden rainstorm.
10. In wet weather, don't leave your golf clubs in the rear deck compartment of your automobile. Excessive moisture can cause your wood clubs to swell.

## ABNORMAL SHOTS

### INTENTIONAL HOOK

1. Use a *closed* stance with the *right* foot placed farther back from the line of flight than the left foot.
2. Move the hands on the grip, more to the *right* than for normal shots.
3. *Close* the club face at address.
4. Keep the hands close to the body on the downswing, and the *right* shoulder *lower* than the *left*.
5. Hit the ball from *inside* the expected line of flight.

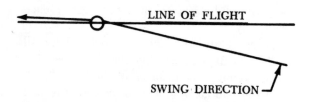

### INTENTIONAL SLICE

1. Use an *open* stance, with the *left* foot placed farther back from the line of flight than the right foot.
2. Move the hands on the grip more to the *left* than for normal shots.
3. *Open* the club face at address.
4. Swing the club from *outside* the expected line of flight.

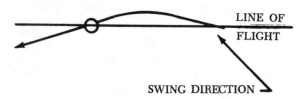

### INTENTIONAL HIGH BALL

1. Play the ball more *forward* off the left foot, to assure impact with the ball when the club head is on the *upswing*. Tee the ball a little higher.
2. At address, the hands should be even with the ball, or slightly behind.
3. *Open* the club face slightly.
4. Use plenty of wrist action, but don't flip the club head at the ball. Also don't lunge at it.

### INTENTIONAL LOW BALL

1. Play the ball more *toward* the *right*, about in the center of the stance.
2. Tee the ball *lower* than usual.
3. At address, the hands should be slightly *ahead* of the ball.
4. *Close* the club face slightly.
5. Hit the ball with a descending stroke, with a full follow-through.
6. Use less wrist action.

### SIDE HILL LIE (ball *above* feet)

1. Shorten the grip on the club handle.
2. Play the ball to the *right* of the target, or open the stance.
3. Play the ball slightly more off the *right* foot.
4. Swing easier, with a shorter backswing than usual.
5. Swing smoothly. Don't fall away from the shot.

### SIDE HILL LIE (ball *below* feet)

1. Stand closer to the ball.
2. Use a slightly *closed* stance, or play the ball to the *left* of the target.
3. Play the ball in the *center* of the stance, with the hands slightly *ahead* of the ball.
4. Keep the weight on the *heels*, with the knees flexed. Stay down to the ball, but don't reach for it.

### UPHILL LIE

1. Use a straighter-faced club than usual, to prevent excess loft in the shot.
2. Keep the weight even on both feet.
3. Play the ball off the "high" foot.
4. Swing along the slope of the hill.
5. Aim to the *right* of the target.
6. Take a practice swing to determine the place where the club head touches the ground.

## DOWNHILL LIE

1. Use a *more lofted club* to get the ball in the air more quickly.
2. Keep the weight even on both feet.
3. Play the ball off the "high" foot.
4. Use a *more upright backswing.*
5. On the downswing, follow the slope of the ground.
6. Take a practice swing to determine the place where the club head touches the ground.
7. Aim to the *left* of the target.

## SAND TRAP SHOTS

### EXPLOSION

1. Set the feet firmly in the sand. Take an open stance, wider than for normal iron shots.
2. Grip the club *low*, and *open* the club face.
3. Play the ball off the *left heel*, and aim to the *left* of the target. *Don't ground the club head* (it is against the rules).
4. Take an exceedingly *upright backswing*, with wrists breaking *sharply.*
5. Keep the left arm straight, and right elbow close to the body.
6. Hit the *sand* from the outside in, about one to two inches *behind* the ball, and *under* it. Don't hit the ball first.
7. *Swing smoothly,* and *follow through completely,* finishing with the hands high. *Don't stub the club head into the sand* and finish with it there.
8. Keep the weight on the left side.

### BURIED BALL

1. Take an *open* stance, with the ball played more *toward* the right foot.
2. Close or hood the club face, with the hands ahead of the ball.
3. Swing harder than usual, and hit the sand *farther behind* the ball.
4. Stay *down* to the shot, and *follow through completely.*

## CHIP SHOT

1. Use a chip shot *only* if the *front lip* of the trap is *low*, and the ball is *sitting up well.* (Never chip off "fluffy" sand.)
2. Use a less lofted club, either a No. 5, 6, 7, or 8 iron, depending on the distance to the flag stick. *Don't use a wedge* for this shot.
3. Grip down on the club handle, and play the ball to the *right of center* of the stance. The stance should be *square* to the line of flight.
4. Hit the ball *cleanly,* taking very little sand *after* the hit. Hit the *ball first.*

## FAIRWAY TRAP

1. Play the shot the same way as for any other fairway shot, provided the front lip of the trap is low enough to clear it.
2. Hit the ball *cleanly,* using either a wood club or an iron, depending upon the distance required to the target.

NOTE: On all trap shots, concentrate on getting out in *one shot.*

## TROUBLE SHOTS

### FROM FAIRWAY DIVOTS

1. Play the ball closer to the *right* foot.
2. Close the club face slightly.
3. Hit *down* on the ball, using plenty of wrist action.
4. Use a more lofted wood club for longer shots.

### FROM DEEP ROUGH

1. Use a well-lofted club (one that will get you out in *one* shot). You may have to sacrifice *some* distance, depending upon the lie of the ball.
2. *Open* the club face wide. Long grass tends to turn the club face in. Play the ball more *toward* the *right* foot.

3. Use an upright swing, and hit down sharply at the ball, with a complete follow-through.
4. Take the shortest route to get the ball back in play. Don't gamble.

## BLASTING FROM WATER

1. If more than an *inch* of water covers the ball, *don't try it.* Drop out, for a one-stroke penalty.
2. Use a pitching wedge. The flat sole of a sand wedge will usually bounce off the water.
3. Hit down sharply, driving the club head into the water, immediately in back of the ball.
4. Don't try for distance. Best success is for an estimated distance of from thirty to forty yards, for a perfect shot.
5. Keep the weight on the *left foot throughout the swing*, and follow through completely.

## HARD GROUND LIES

1. For short distances, try a *sand wedge* to pitch off very hard ground. Grip down on the club handle.
2. Hood the club face slightly to eliminate the chance of bouncing it off the hard ground.
3. Play the shot in a way similar to a sand shot.
4. Hit down sharply, and directly *on* the *back* of the *ball.* Use an *open* stance.
5. Don't quit on the shot, or stub the club head on the ground.
6. *Keep the eye on the ball.*

## FROZEN GROUND LIES

1. Take normal stance, positioning the ball so that it is hit at the *bottom* of the downswing.
2. If using an iron club, *don't hit down on the ball.* "Sweep" it off the ground.

## PUNCH SHOTS

1. When blocked by low-hanging branches, or stymied by several trees which are too close to hit over, or around, use the low punch shot.

2. Use a No. 2 or No. 3 iron, and play the ball opposite the *right* foot. Keep the weight and head to the left throughout the swing.
3. Hood the club face slightly, with the hands *ahead* of the ball.
4. Take a sharp, upright backswing, and hit down crisply. *Stay down,* and *keep the eye on the ball.*

## PITCHING FROM GRASSY BANKS

1. Take stance the same as for other short pitches.
2. Play the ball off the "high" foot, with the weight on the *left* foot.
3. *Open* the club face, and "sweep" the ball up.
4. Swing harder than normal to compensate for a higher trajectory to be expected.
5. Be sure to *hit the ball first,* not the turf behind the ball.
6. In a situation where the flag stick is a considerable distance from the top of the bank, and the ball rests no more than ten to fifteen feet from the top, a chip shot may be employed, using a No. 2 or No. 3 iron. Play the ball to land just short of the green, and bounce on up to the objective.

## THE VALUE OF TRAINING, STUDY, AND PRACTICE

FELLOW GOLFERS:

Have you studied and memorized the simple techniques given in this book? (It is not necessary to memorize the *exact words* of each item, only the principles and most importantly, their sequence.)

Has your teaching professional reviewed your performance?

We keep stressing these points because of their importance in the learning progress and improvement of your golf game.

Whether you choose to use the material in this book, or prefer some other, it is certain that whatever instruction you have received must be firmly fixed in your memory, or it will be of little value to you.

Remember this well-established fact! Most golfers are still trying to learn the game of golf through the *trial-and-error* method. These are the ones who are still trying to break one hundred or ninety, or even those of many years' experience who can't seem to put their game together and break eighty in their score.

The ones who do progress the fastest, and become outstanding players, are those who seek professional instruction on a regular basis, and who *study and practice*. No one can force you to do this. You have to *want* to do it. Golf is a wonderful game from every standpoint, especially when you learn to play it well.

This book was produced not only to help teach you the game of golf, but as a *supplement* to the instructions of your PGA teaching professional, and to help make your game a little more enjoyable.

# SECTION SEVEN

# GOLF EQUIPMENT

What kind of equipment should one acquire when starting to learn this wonderful game of golf?

Certain items are absolutely necessary. Others can be acquired later, as a means of further enhancing the pleasure of playing the game, in addition to helping promote more efficiency in the execution of easy or difficult golf shots.

Collectively, all of these items represent a substantial investment. When this is balanced against the many years of healthful pleasure one receives from their use, however, the dividends far outweigh the investment.

---

THE MOST IMPORTANT ITEMS, AND THE APPROXIMATE PRICE RANGES*:

| | | |
|---|---|---|
| Full set of new and completely balanced golf clubs | | $89.50–$390.00 |
| Starter set, (Nos. 1 and 3 woods, Nos. 3, 5, 7, and 9 irons, and putter) | | $49.50–$ 90.00 |
| Used clubs (complete set reconditioned, or as is) | | $35.00–$150.00 |
| Golf bags (canvas—composition—leather) | | $ 5.95–$175.00 |
| Golf carts | | $19.95–$ 44.95 |
| Golf gloves | | $ 3.00–$ 5.00 |
| Golf shoes (spiked) | | $13.95–$ 42.00 |
| Head covers (for wood club heads) | each | $ 1.50–$ 2.50 |
| Golf balls (new or reconditioned) | each | $ .60–$ 1.30 |
| Golf umbrellas | | $ 7.50–$ 10.00 |
| Golf apparel—rain gear | | as selected |

* All prices shown are subject to changes depending upon the current market.

## GOLF EQUIPMENT

### What to buy?

Of necessity, one of the first things that must be considered by the beginner in golf, of *any* age, is just what equipment is needed to get a good start at learning the game. Naturally, the game cannot be played at all without a few golf clubs and a ball!

In addition to these, one would of course want to think about having a good pair of spiked golf shoes, to help provide a firm footing while executing the golf shots that will be required on various ground surfaces. And other items, such as a bag for the golf clubs, possibly a golf cart to carry them, a golf glove to help in gripping the clubs firmly, and such items of golf apparel as are necessary to help one feel comfortably dressed, and which will permit perfect freedom of movement when swinging the clubs.

But to get back to the matter of golf clubs. What kind should one buy, and how many?

Frankly, the answer depends largely on two major points: how much can you afford to invest, and what does your school instructor or PGA teaching professional think you should have?

Assuming for the moment that the investment in proper equipment will not be an insurmountable problem, let us look at the second point— the teacher's recommendation:

First, we must assume that you have decided to take lessons from a competent instructor, either at your school or from a professional teacher. As we have repeatedly stated, this book will *help* you learn the game. You will still require the services of a good instructor, however, to teach the physical execution of all golf shots. You can't see your own execution, you know!

Second, because of your ability to learn rapidly and make excellent progress, your instructor may see a good future for you in the game. If so, he may recommend that you be properly fitted with a full complement of golf clubs right at the start.

There is no denying that a complete new set of clubs would give any new player a feeling of pride of ownership. By having a full set of all of the required clubs, moreover, the student

will be able to learn the distances he can achieve with each club during his session on the practice range. This becomes mighty important to learn, since it will help him to know what particular club to use for various distances while playing a regular practice round on the golf course, and later on in tournament competition.

For example, let us say that your ball lies in the fairway 140 yards from the green, and you have determined through practice that you can generally achieve this distance with a No. 6 iron. If you did not have one in your set, and had to use a No. 5 iron, you would probably overshoot your objective. If you had used a No. 7, you might end up being too short. Similar situations could occur for other distances.

These are the sort of things to consider when deciding the question of how many clubs to buy. Logically, the person best able to help in this decision is the teacher, who knows just what the student is capable of accomplishing as a result of his performance during lesson periods.

Accordingly, we suggest that *every* golfer contemplating the purchase of a full set of *new* golf clubs give careful consideration to the following advice on pro-fitted golf clubs.

## PRO-FITTED GOLF CLUBS

What kind of golf clubs are you now using?
Are they fitted to your personal requirements?
Is your set of clubs complete for all golf shots you may be required to make?

There are several important factors in the selection of golf clubs for each player. Among them are:

Your athletic and occupational background.
Your physical specifications and aptitudes.
Your temperament.
Your age.
Club quality, length, and weight, shaft flexibility, etc.

These are factors your experienced PGA professional considers in prescribing clubs for *your individual needs*.

For example, most of the time a taller player

needs a longer shaft than a person shorter in height, depending on the length of his arms.

An older person needs a whippy, flexible shaft to help him gain club-head speed for added distance. Also, the swing weight should be carefully chosen for *your individual swing*. This generally applies to the ladies also.

Many golfers, particularly those playing less frequently, are using clubs with *none* of the above individual factors having been considered. Some do not even have a full complement of clubs. This might be all right for a beginner, who buys only a starter set for economy's sake, but sooner or later a *completely balanced* set, fitted to *your* individual requirements, cannot help but improve your game.

## SELECTING THE PROPER CLUB

At the conclusion of Section Three, a chart is shown indicating the average distances which may be attained by the male amateur player, who has learned to execute his golf shots reasonably well. A similar distance chart for women may be found at the conclusion of Section Five.

These distances will be exceeded by many players, particularly by a number of the younger and stronger ones. For some players, however, to attain such distances will be somewhat more difficult.

The important thing to learn is *your individual ability* to achieve certain distances with each club in your golf bag. This can only be accomplished by *regular practice* on the driving range, until you can feel confident of attaining a consistently similar distance for each club every time you use it.

One of the glaring faults of many players is the tendency to underclub. That is, they try to hit a ball farther with the club they select than the distance normally to be expected from it. This of course applies mainly to the various irons.

As long as you have decided to equip yourself with a full set of irons you should choose the one for your golf shot that will attain the required distance without pressing or slugging. The manufacturer made your clubs with a certain loft to the club face for each iron in order to accomplish a certain average distance with that club when it was properly used. To try to get more distance than normally could be expected from it will generally result in trouble.

For example, if you are going to "hood" your 6 iron (tilt the club face forward) for a shot that normally would require a 4 iron, why have a full set of clubs in the first place? Unless you are a magician, moreover, to follow this practice of underclubbing will give you no assurance of *accuracy* in either distance or direction. The player who generally scores well is the one who uses his clubs for the purposes for which they were intended.

## NEW GOLF CLUBS

Complete Sets (for men)

*Matched Woods.* Left, Nos. 1, 2, 3, 4 woods. Right, Nos. 1, 3, 4, 5 woods.

| CLUB FACE LOFTS | AVERAGE NUMBER OF DEGREES | AVERAGE LENGTH |
|---|---|---|
| *Driver* No. 1 | 10–12 | 43 in. |
| *Brassie* " 2 | 13–15 | 42½ " |
| *Spoon* " 3 | 16–18 | 42 " |
| *Cleek* " 4 | 19–21 | 41½ " |
| *Baffy* " 5 | 22–24 | 40¾ " |

For ladies and high-handicap players, we suggest omitting the No. 2 wood and adding a No. 5 wood.

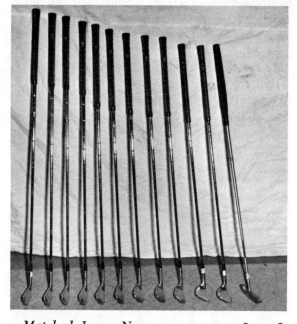

*Matched Irons.* Nos. 1, 2, 3, 4, 5, 6, 7, 8, and 9 irons, pitching wedge, sand wedge, and putter.

| CLUB FACE LOFTS | | AVERAGE NUMBER OF DEGREES | AVERAGE LENGTH |
|---|---|---|---|
| *Driving Iron* | No. 1 | 17 | 39 in. |
| *Mid Iron* | " 2 | 20 | 38½ " |
| *Mid Mashie* | " 3 | 24 | 38 " |
| *Mashie Iron* | " 4 | 28 | 37½ " |
| *Mashie* | " 5 | 32 | 37 " |
| *Spade Mashie* | " 6 | 36 | 36½ " |
| *Mashie Niblic* | " 7 | 40 | 36 " |
| *Pitcher* | " 8 | 44 | 35½ " |
| *Niblic* | " 9 | 49 | 35 " |
| *Pitching Wedge* | | 54 | 34½ " |
| *Sand Wedge* | | 59 | 34½ " |
| *Putter* | | 3 | 34 " |

For tournament play, the legal limit is fourteen clubs in your bag at one time.

See your professional instructor for the correct length of clubs for *your* height and build.

NOTE: All clubs shown are for *right-handed* players. Similar clubs are available for *left-handers.* The No. 1 iron is recommended only for experts.

## CHOICE OF EQUIPMENT

### THE RIGHT BALL

1. The average player, particularly the older one, cannot expect to hit the ball as far as professional tournament players, or low-handicap amateurs.

2. They may use the same highly compressed ball, which is used by these latter players if they wish, but may find that it is too highly compressed for their particular swing.

3. The compression rating for a *high* ball is *85 and up;* for a *medium* ball, *70 to 85;* and for the *low*-compression ball, *70 and under.*

4. Most manufacturers label *high*-compression balls with black brand name and black number.
For *medium*-compression balls—black brand name and red number.
For *low*-compression balls—black brand name and green number. Some have brand and number all in red.

5. For the best results and distance to be attained, choose the ball best suited to *your* particular swing—whether it is *hard, medium,* or *easy.*

6. To qualify this advice, the following explanation may be helpful: At impact, as the club face strikes the back of the ball, it is compressed (pushed in), or "coiled." As it recoils, it actually *rebounds* off the club face, giving added impetus, or momentum to the hit, and to the distance of the ball's flight. This is another reason why a complete follow-through in the swing is so important.
When the player's swing is too easy, the ball cannot be compressed enough for such a recoil. Therefore equal or even more distance may be expected when this player uses a lower compressed ball.

7. Keep in mind that when playing in cold weather, a golf ball has less compression than when it is warm. Many professionals warm

the ball in their hands before putting it into play.

## THE RIGHT CLUB

1. See your teaching professional or school instructor for the kind of shaft and swing weight that suits *your* personal build and ability.

2. For younger or stronger players, capable of hitting the ball *225 yards or more,* a *stiff* shaft, and swing weight *D-0* to *D-5* is best suited for their wood clubs.

3. If your drive averages *200 yards,* use a *regular* shaft, and swing weight of *C-8* to *D-2.*

4. If your drive carries *175 yards,* use a *flexible* shaft, and swing weight of *C-5* to *C-7.*

5. Older players and the ladies usually get the best results using a *flexible* shaft to gain more club-head speed.

## CARE OF YOUR GOLF CLUBS

What is the condition of your golf clubs?
Are the wood club heads nicked or chipped?
Are the grooves of the club faces for both woods and irons filled with dirt?
Are the grips hard and slippery?
(Dirt can affect both swing weight and balance. Hard and slippery grips can cause loss of club control, and loosening of the hands on the grip.)
(Most nicking and chipping of wood club heads can be prevented by the use of *club-head covers.*)

Here are a few simple suggestions:

1. Carry a towel on your golf bag and clean your club heads *after each shot.*

2. Clean your iron club heads with a small fiber brush and soapy water <u>weekly</u>. Then rinse and dry.

3. Wash composition club grips in the same solution.

4. Clean leather grips with naphtha, followed by two light applications of a good leather preservative.

5. Clean wood club heads thoroughly, then apply a good coating of furniture wax and rub until shiny.

6. Don't leave your clubs in the rear deck of your car too long between golfing rounds. Damp weather may cause the wood club heads to swell.

7. See your pro shop for all necessary repairs. It can arrange for expert refinishing of woods, or other repairs requiring competent club repairmen.

8. A good golf bag and cart will help protect your clubs.

## NEW GOLF CLUBS

### For Women

First, let us assume that the average female amateur player is not as strong physically as the average male. There are exceptions, of course, as evidenced by the fact that many women are capable of hitting golf shots for distances equal to, or frequently farther than, those achieved by many men players.

It must be conceded, however, that the majority of women must settle for a shorter distance in their golf shots with the various clubs. Accordingly, some women may find that they can attain more distance with higher-lofted wood clubs than with irons.

For those women who can use wood clubs effectively off the fairway, the higher-lofted clubs, such as the Nos. 5, 6, 7, 8, 9, and 10 woods, may help them accomplish the desired results. We strongly urge them, however, to seek the advice of their school instructor or PGA teaching professional before deciding to use such clubs, instead of the proper iron clubs, which are noted for their accuracy when properly used.

In general, women's clubs should have lighter-weight club heads and the shafts should be more flexible than those used by the average male player, in order to "whip" the club head through the ball faster.

The total swing weight, however, should be determined by the golf instructor, in order to fit the club to the ability of the individual woman player. As a guide, the majority of women will probably find that swing weights of C-6 to C-9 are best suited for their particular swings.

When contemplating the purchase of a new set of clubs, have your professional try your swing with a number of clubs having different shaft flexes and swing weights. The right clubs for you are those with which you can hit the longest and most accurate shots.

## A STARTER SET

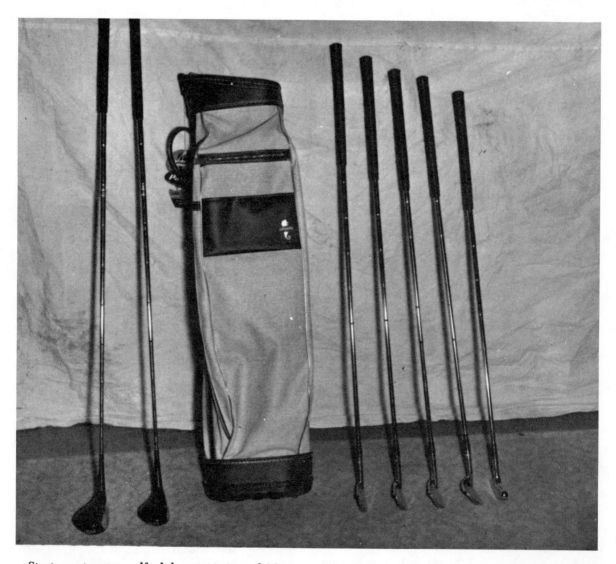

Starter set—*new* golf clubs consisting of Nos. 1 and 3 woods and Nos. 3, 5, 7, and 9 irons and a putter. New canvas golf bag.

For either the male or female beginner, where economy in the investment of golf equipment is often an important factor, a starter set of golf clubs is recommended.

While these sets do not contain all of the clubs required for negotiating the various golf shot distances which one will be faced with, they will enable the average beginner to get along fairly well until a full complement of clubs can be acquired. Prices for these sets are shown at the beginning of this section.

A starter set usually consists of the following clubs:

Nos. 1 and 3 woods
Nos. 3, 5, 7, and 9 irons, and a putter

To this group of clubs, an inexpensive light golf bag should be added to carry the clubs, although in some instances such a bag is included in the price. Later on, when a complete set of new clubs is desired, a reasonable allowance for the initial starter set can be expected.

Starter sets can be purchased in either *new* or *used* clubs. We suggest, however, that in making a selection from either class of clubs, you seek the advice of a professional to assure that the clubs you choose are fitted to *your individual requirements*.

## USED GOLF CLUBS

Used Nos. 1, 3, and 4 woods, Nos. 2, 3, 4, 5, 6, 7, 8, and 9 irons, and pitching wedge or "utility wedge," which combines the pitching and sand wedges. Use your favorite putter.

*New* canvas golf bag (used golf bags are seldom available).

Any pro shop at country clubs, or at municipal and public golf courses, can supply used sets of golf clubs which are *complete for all of the required numbers*. Such clubs may be purchased as is, or fully reconditioned, at various prices, depending on age and quality. An average price range for used golf clubs is given at the beginning of this section. It must be understood that these prices vary at different golf courses depending upon the supply, and the current market for such merchandise.

Occasionally, many players find that they will want to purchase single clubs of various numbers, either woods or irons, which are not included in the set they are presently using. Every pro shop has a club rack containing used golf clubs of every possible kind and number, which can generally be bought at a saving.

When purchasing these clubs we suggest that you have a professional help you in the selection, to assure that the *length of the shaft*, the *flexibility*, and the *swing weight* are correct for your particular needs.

If you buy good-quality used clubs in the beginning, and take good care of them, a liberal allowance may be expected when you are ready to purchase a complete *new* set at a later date.

## ACCESSORIES

### GOLF CARTS

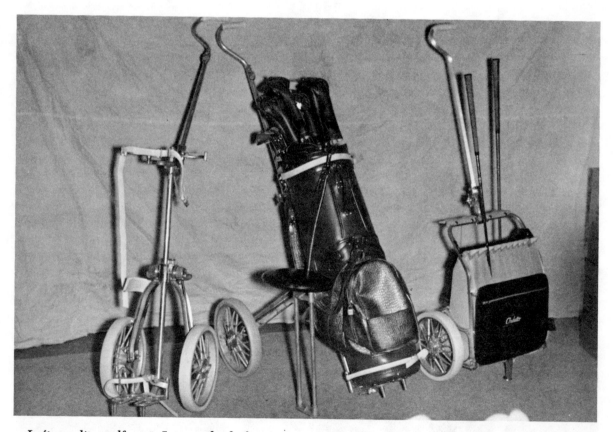

*Left*, quality golf cart. Large wheels for easy rolling.

*Center*, showing quality leather golf bag fitted to deluxe golf cart. Note leather seat mounted on cart, for the comfort-minded golfer.

*Right*, combination cart and club holder. Eliminates the need for a golf bag.

## GOLF BAGS

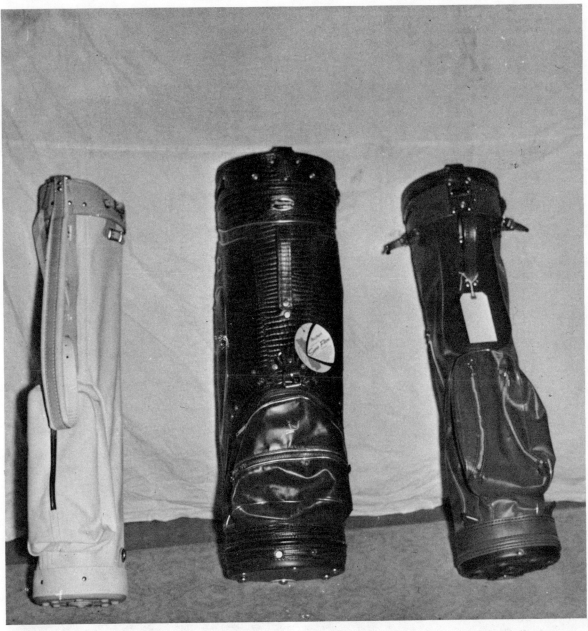

*Left,* light and inexpensive canvas golf bag. Easily carried without golf cart.

*Center,* excellent-quality leather golf bag.

Professional type. These are generally heavier.

*Right,* medium-priced composition material golf bag. Has several large pockets.

## MISCELLANEOUS ACCESSORIES AND APPAREL

*Left rear*, bargain basket—*used* golf balls, re-painted.

*Left center*, club-head covers for woods.

*Left front*, all-leather golf glove, full-fingered.

*Center*, half-fingered golf glove.

*Right rear*, bargain basket—new golf balls, known as X-Outs.

*Right center*, club head covers for irons.

*Front*, new golf balls.

*Right front*, inexpensive golf glove, full-fingered, with nylon back.

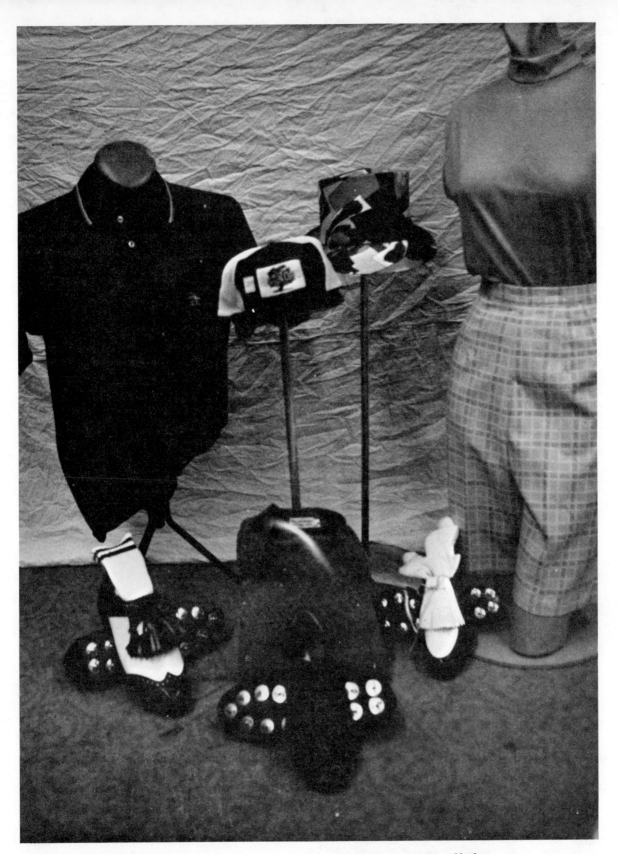

*Left rear*, men's golf shirt.
*Center rear*, golf sweater.
*Center*, men's golf cap.

*Left front*, men's golf shoes.
*Right rear*, ladies' golf shirt and shorts.
*Center rear*, ladies' golf hat and golf shoes.

## CONCLUSION

We have attempted to furnish an instructional textbook, with the execution techniques outlined in such a simple and concise manner that *anyone* can acquire the *basic* knowledge to become a good golfer.

Everything is spelled out in a simple chronology of the things to do in *each phase* of the game. There is no need to read long paragraphs of technical wordage to find the answers to your execution problems.

During the period when the instruction outlines were being prepared, several students, some beginners, and others more experienced, were invited to study the instruction texts, take oral examinations on each phase, and then demonstrate what they had learned in actual practice rounds. The objective was to determine how effective the instruction material in this book was in terms of student training. The tests resulted in consistently lower scores in every instance.

Let us emphasize, however, that neither this book nor any other will *completely* teach you the game of golf. Yes, it will help you to learn the various steps to take—it will put into your mind the things you must do in each situation you are faced with. It will also help you to understand what your school instructor or professional teacher will be telling you.

May we repeat, however, that since you cannot watch your own execution of golf shots, and particularly for those whose performance (in spite of their knowledge of the text) may not be quite correct, by all means seek professional instruction on a *regular* basis in the physical execution of all golf shots.

To you, and to every golfer for whom this book was written, the authors extend their best wishes for outstanding success in the most wonderful game the world has ever known:

GOLF!

## QUIZ FOR STUDENTS

### Sample Form

#### THE STANDARD GRIP

Give the four steps of the grip in the proper order.

State why you perform each step.

#### SQUARE, OPEN, AND CLOSED STANCES

Explain and demonstrate each stance.

Explain how and why each is used.

#### STANCE AND ADDRESS (the tee shot)

Outline the fourteen items involved in the stance and address in the proper order.

Demonstrate, and give the reasons for each item.

#### THE BACKSWING

Outline the fifteen items for the backswing in the proper order.

Demonstrate, and give the reasons for each item.

#### THE DOWNSWING

Outline the nine items for the downswing in the proper order.

Demonstrate, and give the reasons for each item.

#### IMPACT AND FOLLOW-THROUGH

State the five items involved in the impact and follow-through in the proper order.

Demonstrate, and give the reasons for each item.

#### GOLF TERMS

How many of the golf terms outlined in this book can you name?

What do they mean?

#### GOLF ETIQUETTE

Outline the twelve items listed in this book.

Give reasons why these items are important.

With either oral or written tests, the important thing is to determine the student's knowledge of each subject, then proceed with the physical execution training.